MY ROSARY JOURNAL

"Let us resolve to pray to the Blessed Virgin especially with the recitation of the Rosary. Mary will reign in our heart and if Mary is with us, what can we fear? With Mary's love in our heart we shall attain eternal salvation."

Rev. James Alberione, SSP

My Rosary Journal

The Great Mysteries

William F. Maestri

Illustrations by
Marilyn Carter Rougelot

ALBA · HOUSE   NEW · YORK

SOCIETY OF ST. PAUL, 2187 VICTORY BLVD., STATEN ISLAND, NY 10314

Produced and designed in the United States of America by the
Fathers and Brothers of the Society of St. Paul,
2187 Victory Boulevard, Staten Island, New York 10314,
as part of their communications apostolate.

ISBN: 0-8189-0673-1

Printing Information:

Current Printing - first digit	1	2	3	4	5	6	7	8	9	10

Year of Current Printing - first year shown

1993	1994	1995	1996	1997	1998	1999	2000

Contents

Introduction / ix

THE JOYFUL MYSTERIES

THE ANNUNCIATION / 3
 Woman of Courageous Faith / 5
 Woman for God — Woman for Others / 6

THE VISITATION / 9
 Love in Action / 11
 Leap for Joy / 12

THE NATIVITY / 15
 Fear Not / 16
 Lost in Wonder / 18

THE PRESENTATION / 21
 Sign of Contradiction / 23
 They Returned / 24

THE FINDING OF JESUS IN THE TEMPLE / 27
 Why? / 29
 Wisdom, Age, Grace / 31

THE SORROWFUL MYSTERIES

THE AGONY IN THE GARDEN / 37
 Pray / 38
 This Chalice / 39

THE SCOURGING / 43
    Pilate Took Jesus / 43
    Scourged Him / 45

CROWNING WITH THORNS / 49
    Hail King! / 49
    Ecce Homo / 51

CARRYING THE CROSS / 55
    Weep Not For Me / 55
    Toward Golgotha / 57

THE CRUCIFIXION / 61
    Forgiveness / 62
    It Is Consummated / 64

THE GLORIOUS MYSTERIES

THE RESURRECTION / 69
    To See the Tomb / 70
    He Is Risen... Go and Tell! / 72

THE ASCENSION / 75
    Wait / 76
    Looking Up / 78

PENTECOST / 81
    Humble Beginning / 83
    Tongues of Fire / 85

THE ASSUMPTION / 89
    On Earth as in Heaven / 90
    Hope / 92

CORONATION / 95
    Fully Human / 97
    Full of Grace / 98

EPILOGUE

The Rosary: A School of Prayer / 101

Introduction

MY EARLY RELIGIOUS IMAGINATION was formed in the immigrant, pre-Vatican II Catholic Church. Without wanting to idealize the past, I am grateful to the Church of that historical moment. Likewise, I am appreciative of the renewal called for by the Second Vatican Council. I am hopeful in that Spirit which lures the Church into a future yet to be. Since I am a child of that immigrant, pre-Vatican II Church, one of my first religious memories involves the Rosary. To be specific, the Rosary of my grandmother. And not just any Rosary. This Rosary actually glowed in the dark! To a little boy (without television, mind you) this was awesome and only added to the mystery.

"Why does your Rosary glow in the dark?" I remember asking my grandmother, unable to take my eyes off that Rosary. My grandmother smiled at me and took her Rosary in her fingers and held it up.

"I say my Rosary while I'm waiting to fall asleep," she said. "Sometimes I wake up in the middle of the night and, because it glows, I am able to find my Rosary easily in the dark. After a few minutes I fall right back to sleep."

This quaint little story from long ago contains a timeless lesson — namely, the Rosary continues to be found by new generations of Catholics. The Rosary endures as a source of spiritual strength, comfort, and wisdom to those who find themselves searching for peace amid the darkness. In fact, the Rosary has enjoyed a revival in recent times as a form of popular piety. No doubt much of this current revival has to do with world events. More and more we are coming to see that the Rosary is, and has long been, one of the most popular forms of prayer for peace. This is most ironic for one of the frequent criticisms leveled at the Rosary is the charge that praying the Rosary is "too individualistic and pietistic." One frequently hears it said that the Rosary removes the Christian from "the concerns and events of our everyday world." Yet this is not the case.

Those who use the Rosary as a form of praying for world peace are keenly aware of world events. In addition, those who pray the Rosary for world peace have a profound *understanding* of world events and history. To pray the Rosary for peace is to acknowledge that God is *active* in the world and in human history. God does not passively watch from afar. God is present, luring us to deeper faith, love, justice, hope, and peace. Obviously this is anything but individualistic and being removed from the larger world.

Furthermore, the Rosary persists because of its power to illuminate and guide us through the mystery of our human existence. The Great Mysteries of the Rosary are fundamentally about God's encounter with our humanity through the lives of Jesus and Mary. The Great Mysteries of the Rosary do not cancel our humanity; rather, they help us to be more fully human by being more attentive to the grace of God. As we pray the Rosary and meditate on the Great Mysteries, we become ever mindful that Mary and Jesus were fully human. They shared our humanity and revealed the ways in which God's grace enables us to live in a manner which is fully alive. The Great Mysteries of the Rosary are anything but an escape from the human condition. These Great Mysteries challenge us to be responsive to the God who comes to us in joy and sorrow. These Great Mysteries hold out to us the challenge to be born anew through the glorious power of the Holy Spirit. The Great Mysteries of joy, sorrow, and glory illuminate the full spectrum of human experience. At the birth of a child, the suffering and death of a loved one, and the rush of the Spirit which dispels our fears, the Great Mysteries remind us that God's grace is ever present. We never face life and death and the beyond alone.

There is something typically Catholic about the Rosary for the Rosary is not just a series of prayers. It is a physical object which we can touch. We not only pray the Rosary, but we hold and finger in our hand the cross, medal, and beads that make up the tangible Rosary. Catholicism is a story which affirms the basic goodness of the tangible. Objects — bread, wine, candle, cross, oil, water, and Rosary — remind us of the deep mysteries which exist beyond our five senses. It is through these objects — these sacraments — that we can experience God's gracious presence. The tangible is a help in keeping us focused on the world to come.

The Great Mysteries of the Rosary are typically Catholic in another sense —namely they lend themselves to artistic expression. Throughout history numerous artists have found inspiration in the Great Mysteries of the Rosary. I am honored to introduce the religious illustrations of Marilyn Carter Rougelot. She is a well known and highly respected artist who now turns her talents to the religious dimension. It is most fitting that for her initial offering Ms. Rougelot would select the Great Mysteries of the Rosary. I know that you will find her work as inspiring, attractively human, and spiritual as I have.

This little book was not meant to substitute for the Rosary. Rather, it is intended to be an ongoing companion to the Rosary. The format is simple. There are three major sections corresponding to the Joyful, Sorrowful, and Glorious Mysteries. Under each major section are the Five Great Mysteries along with two aspects of each Mystery for further reflection. A brief meditation accompanies each of the Great Mysteries, based on the appropriate illustration. After each meditation there are a series of reflection questions based on the Great Mystery itself as well as the accompanying illustration. The two aspects which further develop each Great Mystery also contain a brief meditation, along with questions for further reflection. Space is provided for writing one's own reflections.

This book is not just a collection of illustrations and a series of reflections by the author on the Great Mysteries. It is a personal journal. This book belongs to each of *you*. It is *your* reflection on the Great Mysteries of God's unbounded love revealed through Jesus and Mary. The Rosary itself is an ongoing journey into our humanity, the mystery of daily life, and the gracious presence of God. We don't simply pray the Rosary and meditate on the Great Mysteries. We live them as disciples of Jesus, inspired by the life of Mary.

Too often gratitude can be expressed by the author of a book as a mere polite requirement. Such is not the case with this book by this author. I am grateful to my long deceased but not forgotten grandmother, Hazel C. Maestri, who gave me a love for the Rosary. There have been many times — and may it be so in the future — when I was able to find the Rosary in the midst of darkness.

The spiritual and artistic value of this book has been greatly enhanced through the illustrations of Marilyn Carter Rougelot. Her work and our many conversations have enriched my love for the Great Mysteries.

The manuscript was typed with great care by Doctor Joan Doyle, a retired professor of history at St. John's University, New York and currently a member of the staff of the Elderhostel Program at St. Joseph Abbey. In addition, Dr. Doyle enhanced the quality of this work by her thoughtful suggestions and observations. I am grateful for her generosity and competence in preparing this manuscript for publication.

Finally, I am grateful to Alba House for its willingness to bring this book to publication. Over the years I have enjoyed an excellent professional relationship with the Society of St. Paul community on Staten Island. Most importantly, I have been enriched by the friendship and support of Father Edmund Lane, Brother Aloysius Milella, and Father Victor Viberti. I am grateful that I can contribute to their important ministry of evangelization through various forms of communication. May the Spirit continue to guide their work for the Gospel.

William F. Maestri
St. Joseph Abbey
St. Benedict, Louisiana
Immaculate Conception 1992

The Joyful Mysteries

WHY DON'T CHRISTIANS look more redeemed?" This pointed question — an accusation really — was posed by a young boy to his sister after attending one of their father's Sunday worship services. The boy was Frederick W. Nietzsche who, in time, would become the leading philosopher of modern existential atheism. It was Nietzsche who declared, "God is dead!" We can only wonder: if his early religious experience had been more joyful, would things have been different? Of course we will never know. But one thing we *do* know: the Christian life is not about the forming of gloomy saints. Rather, the Christian life is about joy. Not the joy of "Have a nice day" superficiality. Christian joy flows from the indwelling Holy Spirit. Such a Spirit-filled joy does not excuse us from the cross. However, Christian joy accepts the cross as the way into eternal life.

It is most appropriate that we begin our reflections on the Great Mysteries of the Rosary with Christian joy, for the Joyful Mysteries invite us into the joy of faith. Such joy in faith comes from the grace to experience in our everyday lives the unbounded love of God. Joy in faith frees us to live for God and others in this world with our hearts set on the world to come. Hence, to be joyful is not to withdraw from life but to draw more deeply from it "the deep down things" of God. The joy in faith allows us to see in the ordinary events of life, as well as in those times of great testing, that we are not alone. God is with us and for us.

The Joyful Mysteries invite us into the joy of faith. And wonderfully human Mary is our guide. For in these five mysteries we see the joy of faith in action. From the Annunciation to the Finding of Jesus in the Temple, Mary is invited to journey ever deeper into the mystery of God's love. This journey is not without its anxiety, confusion, trials, and cross: Mary is troubled by the words of the messenger from God. There is no room in the inn when it is time for Jesus to be born. The prophet Simeon tells Mary that a sword will pierce her heart. Mary is told early on by Jesus that he must be about his Father's work. He will not be with her forever. Yet, in the face of all these challenges, Mary can proclaim: "Behold, I am the servant of the Lord; let it be done unto me according to your word..." "My soul magnifies the Lord, and my spirit rejoices in God my Savior..." (Lk 1:38, 46-47).

How can Mary say these words? The answer is to be found in the joy of faith — faith in the one who never disappoints and in the Spirit who gives a joy which no one can take away.

1

The Annunciation

Luke 1:26-38

LIFE WRITES ITS LESSONS, learned and unlearned, upon the face. If we dare to look deeply into a mirror and not forget what we see, there is a story revealed about how we live. It seems as if the face, especially the eyes, serve as a window into the soul. To look deeply into another is uncomfortable because of its revelation. Only the look of love can ease the fear and open the heart to God, self, and others.

Dare to look into Mary's face. What do you see? The eyes reveal so much. We see a young woman who is "greatly troubled." It is an awesome thing to be called by the Lord for a special work in history. And what a special work it will be! Mary will provide the human face of God. Luke tells us Mary "considered in her mind" what the words of Gabriel might mean. However it is not in the mind, in human reason, that Mary will come to the power of this mystery of grace. It is only through trust that the Word becomes flesh and the victory of grace over sin takes its decisive turn.

Look deeply into the eyes of Mary. What do you see? This "greatly troubled" young woman is also "the handmaid of the Lord." We see in her eyes, shining through the fear, the spirit of trust. Everything is not clear but this does not stop Mary from believing. Deep in Mary's eyes there shines out a joy which comes from amazing grace. Living within her is the good news of salvation and the hope of the world. Mary will leave in haste to be with Elizabeth. Good news must be shared and Life must touch life.

Spend a few moments in quiet reflection. Meditate on the story of the Annunciation in the Gospel of Luke (1:26-38). Likewise, meditate on the illustration of the Annunciation. Write your responses to the questions below.

How is the humanity of Mary brought forth in the illustration of the Annunciation?

_____

_____

_____

How has the humanity of Mary inspired you to be more open to God's word?

_____

_____

_____

Have there been times when you were troubled by having to put God's word into practice?

_____

_____

_____

What have you found to be a major obstacle to living God's word? How has Mary's Annunciation been a source of strength?

_____

_____

_____

How does Mary's humble background help her to be open to the Lord's word? In what ways have you struggled with humility?

_____

_____

_____

Woman of Courageous Faith

In the Gospel of St. Luke women play a prominent role. Women follow Jesus as He goes about preaching the Kingdom (Lk 8:1-3). Women such as Martha and Mary offer Jesus hospitality (Lk 10:38-42). Women provide the earliest testimony of Jesus' resurrection (Lk 24:1-11). And in the first of the Joyful Mysteries, the Annunciation, Luke presents Mary as a woman of courageous faith.

On first reflection it can seem strange to speak of Mary's courageous faith. After all, she is a young woman and by her own admission "a lowly handmaid" (Lk 1:47). Luke tells us that Mary was "deeply disturbed" by the words of the angel Gabriel (Lk 1:29). Even the angel Gabriel recognizes Mary's fear as he goes on to announce God's plan for salvation (Lk 1:29). Hence the question, How can we speak of Mary's courageous faith?

The answer lies in the Beatitudes — to be specific, "Blest are the pure of heart for they shall see God" (Mt 5:8). Purity of heart should not be restricted to sexuality and violations of the Sixth and Ninth Commandments. Rather, purity of heart denotes a radical centering or focusing of one's whole life in the will of God. Purity of heart is to will one thing with one's whole being. Purity of heart can be experienced by anyone who must accomplish a crucial work or give a performance which requires great concentration. The performer or athlete is able to block out everything except the attainment of the goal.

So it is with Mary. Her heart is so pure because she wills one thing completely — to do God's will. Yet she is troubled, fearful, and confused. Yes, she initially feels the tension of doubt: "How can this be since I do not know man?" (Lk 1:34). This clearly reveals a quite human response. However grace builds on human nature: "I am the servant of the Lord. Let it be done to me as you say" (Lk 1:38). These words are courageous; they come from the heart. These words resound with a faith that does not completely understand but does completely trust: "My being proclaims the greatness of the Lord, my spirit finds joy in God my savior..." "God who is mighty has done great things for me..." (Lk 1:46, 49).

Spend a few moments in quiet reflection. As you do, pray the first decade of the Rosary, focusing on Mary's willingness to trust completely in God's word. Write your responses to the following questions.

List some of the women you know who have influenced you by their courageous faith. Give one example of their faith.

_____

_____

What daily concerns and temptations keep you from doing God's will? How have you confronted these challenges?

_____

_____

What recent incident has challenged your faith? Were you able to respond with courage? Explain.

_____

_____

Write a brief prayer on your need for purity of heart. In addition to reflecting on your life experiences, prayerfully read Mary's Canticle (Lk 1:46-55).

_____

_____

Woman for God — Woman for Others

The Christian dynamic of love is threefold: love of God, love of neighbor, and love of self. And the order of this is crucial! Mary first of all was a woman totally in love with God. Her being is animated by her love for the gracious God who has done great things in her. Mary is the woman for God. It is this love for God which frees her to overcome the anxiety and confusion that might have kept her from trusting the angel. It is this love for God, no doubt formed in her family from the first, which allowed Mary to be the human instrument for our salvation.

It is this total love for God which empowers Mary to be the woman for others. Christian love seeks first of all the love of God. However, such a love is always extended outward toward those in need. The Annunciation of Mary will lead to the Visitation; Mary's good news makes room for the joyful realization that Elizabeth is to bear a child. The love of God does not isolate us from others. It should never make us feel superior to or above others. Rather, God's love is expansive and moves us in solidarity with and for others.

Finally, we are moved to love ourselves in the proper way. That is, because we love God and because we can be for others, we are empowered to acknowledge who we are — the

6

redeemed children of God. Like Mary, we too can exclaim, "My being proclaims the greatness of the Lord... for He who is mighty has done great things for me and holy is His name" (Lk 1:46-49). We can love ourselves in the proper way because we are loved by God without reservation.

Spend a few moments in quiet reflection. Center your thoughts and feelings on some recent and important experiences of love. Write your responses to the questions below.

Think of a recent experience in which the love of God filled your heart. Try to describe how you felt. Did this experience change you in any way? How?

_____

_____

_____

How has God's love helped you to be more concerned for the needs of others? Give an example.

_____

_____

_____

What prevents you from experiencing God's love? Fear? Unworthiness? How does this keep you from loving yourself in the right way?

_____

_____

_____

Do you struggle with the pain of self-rejection? Write a prayer in the space below in which you tell Mary of this pain and of how God's grace can heal you.

_____

_____

_____

7

The Visitation

Luke 1:39-56

WHAT A WONDERFULLY HUMAN GIFT is the sense of touch and the power of another's hand. We touch to support, reassure, direct, protect, and correct. The holding of hands is an especially human and sacramental sign. The hands of mother and child fit with the firm tenderness that conveys care and direction. The hands of bride and groom come together to express the fidelity of their passion. We seek the hand of the sick and the dying to assure them they are not forgotten.

The hands of Mary and Elizabeth meet in the sharing of their good news. Inside both women the Almighty has done great things. It is the only human thing to do — touch the life that leaps in the womb for joy. One can hear Elizabeth saying to Mary, "The baby in my womb kicked with joy at your voice." We can see Mary drawing close to Elizabeth. We can see Elizabeth placing Mary's hands in hers and resting them on her abdomen. There is the human need to touch and communicate about the mystery of life in ways beyond words.

Mary's Visitation to Elizabeth is a sign of God's visiting his people. In the Incarnation God touches our humanity so deeply that He becomes human in Jesus. God does not visit us in an abstract way. The Word becomes flesh (Jn 1:14). God takes us into his hands, not in anger but in life-giving love (Ps 31:15).

Luke tells us that Mary stayed with Elizabeth for about three months and then returned home. Every visit bespeaks a leaving. Mary must return to prepare for the birth of Jesus. In time, Mary will touch the human flesh of her child and her whole being will rejoice in God the Savior.

Spend a few moments in prayerful meditation on the Visitation in the Gospel of Luke (1:39-56). After your scriptural meditation, reflect on the illustration of the Visitation. Write your responses to the questions below.

9

After reflecting on the illustration of the Visitation, write a meditation (prayer or poem) on the human encounter between Mary and Elizabeth.

_____

_____

_____

_____

_____

_____

What important aspects of our humanity are brought forth in the Visitation?

_____

_____

_____

How does God's grace shine through these human aspects of the Visitation?

_____

_____

_____

What was the most recent example of your visiting someone in need? Were you able to be an instrument of God's grace? How?

_____

_____

_____

Are you able to receive the visitation of others who come in response to your needs? Explain.

_____

_____

_____

Love in Action

Pain shrinks our world and narrows our perceptions. We turn inward and focus on our hurt. Pain becomes a prison which locks us in solitary confinement and places the NO VISITORS sign around our neck. By contrast, the joy of good news draws us into the larger world of God and others. We *must* find someone to tell or we feel we will burst. When we come into good news our perceptions are enriched and the size of our world is enlarged many times over. Good news moves us to touch others.

The deepest of joys and the best of good news is the experience of being loved in a totally accepting and non-judgmental way. Such is God's love for us. Such is the Love who comes to be born in Mary. And the good news of this love must be shared with another. Mary, after her Annunciation, goes in haste to be with Elizabeth (Lk 1:39). Love is not an idea to be contemplated or endlessly refined through philosophical speculation. Love is a verb — an action in which we risk revealing ourselves by affecting the world around us. Likewise, love is the willingness to be affected by others. Christian love in action is not mindless, compulsive, egoistic behavior. Christian love is the life of action in which we bring the joy of the Gospel to the world.

Mary went to Elizabeth out of love and joy. It would have been easier for Mary to remain in Nazareth. It would have been much more befitting Mary's place in salvation history to wait for Elizabeth to visit her. Yet all such purely egoistic considerations vanish. Love acts from the heart in order to see with the mind (Blondel). And what do we see? In Mary's Visitation we see human love revealing the power of the divine. For God, the God who is Love, is about to visit His people. The time of great joy is near at hand. The hour of unexpected grace is about to dawn.

Spend a minute in quiet reflection on the Visitation. When your reflections are complete, pray the second decade of the Rosary. Center your thoughts on Mary visiting Elizabeth and God visiting us in the coming of Jesus. Write your responses to the questions below.

When you receive good news, who is the first person with whom you want to share the joy?

_____

_____

_____

How has God recently visited you with His grace?

_____

_____

_____

In what ways have you been an instrument of God's grace in visiting others?

_____

_____

_____

Who are those special people who need a visit from you and whom you need to visit (relative, friend, the sick, or someone with whom you are at odds)?

_____

_____

_____

Leap for Joy

Luke, a physician as well as an evangelist, tells us that "when Elizabeth heard the greeting of Mary, the baby leaped in her womb" (Lk 1:41). We might dismiss this as simple piety or as a religious figure of speech used to highlight the importance of the moment. Yet there is a deep truth which would appeal to Luke as a physician and evangelist: all human life, at whatever stage of existence, is attentive to God and finds joy in the Lord of life. Even at an early age God's grace is able to influence our development. Modern medical science attests to the importance of prenatal influence on the human being developing in the womb. Prenatal medical science tells us that the relationship between mother and unborn child is crucial. The joy of the Spirit which filled Elizabeth rushed through her body and caused her baby to jump with joy.

The same Spirit which rushed through Elizabeth at the Visitation will abide in John the Baptizer throughout his mission. In the presence of Jesus and the Spirit there is a profound joy and zest which moves our whole being. This is not to say that we live without conflict and suffering. We know that John will dare to speak truth to power and confront the moral smugness of the self-righteous. He will be put to death for Jesus and the Gospel. Yet he dies, and even lives, as a man who leaped for joy throughout his life because of Jesus.

The mission of the Church, and of the individual Christian, is to leap for joy and bring Jesus to the world. Through prayer Mary visits us and once again points to Jesus our Savior. That same Spirit which rushed through Elizabeth and moved John to leap is ours through Baptism. Let it be said of us that daily we leap with joy in the Spirit as we proclaim Jesus. Let us visit one another and join together, going forth to tell the world of the mighty love of God.

Spend a few moments in quiet reflection. Center your meditation of the expression of joy. Use Luke 1:41-46 as a biblical source for reflection. Write your response to the following questions.

Think of a recent experience of joy. How did you experience God's grace? Are you able to express joy in your spirituality? How?

_____

_____

Do you bring joy to others through your living of the Gospel? Give an example. What keeps you from showing the joy you feel?

_____

_____

In what ways have you proclaimed the Gospel in imitation of John the Baptizer?

_____

_____

Even when you experience opposition for living the Gospel, are you able to express a greater sense of joy in the Spirit? Explain.

_____

_____

_____

The Nativity

Luke 2:1-19

C HRISTMAS VESPERS ANTIPHON beautifully captures the mystery of the Nativity: "O, Wondrous Exchange!" For this is exactly what the birth of Jesus is — the wondrous exchange between God and man; the divine and the human. And what more powerful way to express this mysterious exchange of unbounded love than with the birth of a child.

With the birth of Jesus, God touches our humanity so deeply that the Word becomes flesh (Jn 1:14). But we do not passively watch God's love become visible in Jesus. We reach out and upward in order to respond to the God who touches us. We must confirm this wondrous exchange.

God's loving touch of our humanity is powerfully expressed with the birth of Jesus. The pain of childbirth gives way to the joy of a newborn son. Mary forgets the rejection, the surroundings, and the violence as she looks into the face of her child. She lovingly caresses his head and holds him close to her breast. The baby instinctively reaches out to the soft sounds of his mother's voice. The eyes are not yet in focus. The newborn depends on hearing and touch. The baby reaches out to the sound of love. The small hand traces the face of love. Before love appears to the eye, it comes to us in sound and touch.

Who cannot identify with Joseph? There is a special intimacy between mother and child which fathers will never know. In a profound sense fathers find themselves looking on, rather than looking into the mystery of birth. Yet Joseph is present and his face and touch will have their time in the life of this child. For now, Joseph is strong through his silence. His loving presence is wise enough to leave space for Mary and Jesus.

Spend a few moments in prayerful meditation on the Nativity in the Gospels of Matthew (2:1-12) and Luke (2:1-14). When your scriptural reflections are completed, meditate on the illustration of the Nativity. Write your responses to the questions below.

After meditating on the illustration of the Nativity, what human emotions become present?

_____

_____

How does the human birth of Jesus reflect the unbounded love of God for us?

_____

_____

Does the human birth of Jesus strengthen your growth in the spiritual life? How?

_____

_____

What do you think was going through the mind and feelings of Joseph?

_____

_____

What does Joseph's silent presence teach us about love? Intimacy? Fatherly love? Family life? How does Joseph reveal God's continuing love for us?

_____

_____

Fear Not

How strange to talk about fear as we meditate on the Joyful Mysteries and the deepest of these Mysteries — the Nativity. Yet on closer reflection we see that joy and fear are not antagonistic, but complementary. However, we must make a careful distinction between the fear which moves us away from God and the fear which evolves in us a sense of God's majestic power.

The story of the Fall in Genesis tells us that one of the first consequences of sin is fear. God searches the Garden for Adam but he hides. God finally confronts Adam. God wants to know why Adam was in hiding. Adam responds, "I heard you in the Garden and I was afraid because I was naked; and I hid myself" (Gn 3:10). Sin evokes fear and fear makes us flee the presence of God. Our pride, the basis of all sin, does not want us to be seen by God. We don't want to be a creature in the presence of our Creator. Pride tells us we are inferior and unworthy. Pride moves us to grasp for that which is beyond our reach; and we fall. In the Fall, we take flight from the One who alone can save. Yet we run away. Fear will not allow us to believe in the healing power of God's forgiving love.

Yahweh does not give up on us or the power of His love. Luke tells us that shepherds were tending their flocks. Suddenly "an angel of the Lord appeared to them, and the glory of the Lord shone around them..." (Lk 2:9). And what was the shepherds' response? They were filled with fear. Hence the angel's proclamation: "Be not afraid... I bring you good news of a great joy which will come to all people... to you is born a Savior, Christ the Lord" (Lk 2:10-11). Once again God comes looking for us. We are not to flee out of fear. We are to be filled with joy at the Good News — the Savior is born to us. Down through the centuries God has been searching for us. We have been in flight. Now the chase is over. And to our surprise the glory of God is *not* our condemnation but the message of peace. We no longer need to hide. Love drives out fear. In God's presence we can be seen for who we are — the beloved of God.

Spend a few moments in quiet reflection. If possible, turn down the lights and allow the image of the Nativity to surface. Imagine that you are present with the shepherds. Write your responses in the space below.

If you had been present with the shepherds to whom the birth of Jesus was announced, what might have been your response?

_____

_____

In what ways have you tried to hide from God? Why were you afraid?

_____

_____

How has God's love and a human love been able to free you from your fear?

_____

_____

17

What fear in your life would you like to give to the newborn Jesus?

_____

_____

Imagine you are being drawn into that stable where Jesus was born. Write a prayer, poem, or hymn which expresses your sense of awe at God's power.

_____

_____

Lost in Wonder

Rabbi Abraham Joshua Heschel once wrote: "Among the many things that religious tradition holds in store for us is *a legacy of wonder*. The surest way to suppress our ability to understand the meaning of God and the importance of worship is *to take things for granted*. Indifference to the sublime wonder of living is the root of sin." And what does it mean to wonder? Wonder is radical amazement at the gift and mystery of existence. The basic reality of existence evokes in us wonder, radical amazement, that there is something rather than nothing.

The sense of wonder is difficult for modern man. Our perceptions are structured according to the rules of evidence by way of science. We rush about organizing our experience into patterns which can be explained, predicted, and controlled by the powers of human reason. The more we structure

our perceptions, that which we see by the rules of science, the more wonder recedes into the background. We find it hard to give thanks, to be eucharistic, when we come to believe that everything is the work of our hands. The loss of wonder traps us in a one-dimensional world of our making. Creation no longer speaks to us of the grandeur of God.

The Nativity of the Word into human flesh calls for the deepest sense of wonder. To be drawn into the birth of Jesus is to be radically amazed at the unbounded love of God. For the transcendent, wholly Other comes into our human condition in the most radical of ways — God becomes our flesh. The modern expectation is for the wildly spectacular and the highly visible which overwhelms. But when we look into the manger we are lost in wonder at the sublime wisdom of God. In the powerlessness of this child we see the power of God. The distance of the God above is bridged by love in this child here below. We must raise our voices in joyful praise:

Cry out unto God all the earth Sing of the glory of His name, Make His praise glorious: Sing unto God: How sublime are your works. (Psalm 66:2-3)

Find a quiet place for meditation. Spend time meditating on the gift of existence — in particular, *your* existence. Write your responses to the questions below.

Think of a recent instance when you were filled with wonder. What are the things and who are the people who evoke wonder in you? Why?

_____

_____

In what ways have you taken the gift of life for granted?

_____

_____

What aspects of modern life have kept us from developing a sense of wonder?

_____

_____

How does my participation in the Eucharist foster a sense of wonder?

_____

_____

When you meditate on the Nativity what feelings do you experience? Write a brief prayer in response to these feelings (see Psalm 139:14).

_____

_____

The Presentation

Luke 2:22-40

E VERY HUMAN JOY, no matter how deep or lasting, contains the seeds of sorrow. Perhaps this is because we realize that in this world the glory and joy pass away. In the words of the existential philosopher Camus, there is a "cruel mathematics which claims our condition." At some level of our being we are aware of the temporality and finitude of all that is. Each day we must fight back the feelings of despair. Each day we must be renewed in hope.

One of the deepest of human joys is the birth of a child. This is especially true for the mother who bonds in the most profound of ways. The joy and intimacy of giving birth also bespeaks the reality of separation and independent existence. Every mother must let go of her child if that child is to become a mature human being. How great is the temptation to hold on. How powerful is the hurt that letting go demands.

Mary and Joseph present Jesus in the Temple in accordance with the law. Yet in the midst of this routine demand something extraordinary happens. Simeon takes Jesus from Mary and proclaims that this child is the Savior of the world. Jesus' mission and destiny lies beyond the control of Mary and Joseph. This child is "a light of revelation to the Gentiles, and of glory to God's people Israel" (Lk 2:32).

The presentation of Jesus begins the long process of Mary and Joseph's relinquishing this child. There is a deep joy at the words of Simeon and Anna. This child will be about the Lord's work. At the same time we see the hand of Mary, like any loving mother, wanting to hold on. Yet her deeper love moves Mary to give Jesus to the world.

Spend a few minutes in quiet prayer. Read carefully the story of the presentation of Jesus in the Temple. Write your responses to the following questions.

21

Write about a recent example of your experiencing great joy. Did you also experience a sense of sorrow? Explain.

_____

_____

_____

_____

Write about a recent experience when you were required to relinquish something or someone you love. How does this Joyful Mystery relate to your experience?

_____

_____

_____

_____

Reflect on the illustration of the Presentation of Jesus. What do you think is going through Mary's mind as she hears the words of Simeon and Anna?

_____

_____

_____

_____

How do you spiritually cope with loss in your life? Does prayer help you to see a deeper form of faith and love? Explain.

_____

_____

_____

_____

Sign of Contradiction

The Presentation of Jesus in the Temple challenges a fundamental belief of the modern world. We moderns, too often intoxicated with our own power and puffed up by the work of our hands, believe that we are the masters of our fate and the sole authors of all that is. We find it hard, if not absurd, to admit of any power beyond *this* world. Increasingly, through queries and technology, we close the windows onto that other world. We turn away from the deeper dimensions of existence. We settle for the here and now. We close ourselves to that grace which reveals the depth of God's love below the surface. Having come of age, we tell ourselves we have outgrown God. To the modern mind, the creature has become the creator.

The Presentation of Jesus in the Temple stands in contradiction to our modern self-congratulations and liberation. The Presentation of Jesus to God says this: we are not here because of our own making and willing. All life is a gift from our gracious God. To present Jesus to the Lord is a profound reminder of our origin and destiny — life in God. We are not our own. We belong to Another. We will render an account of our stewardship to Him. None of this is cause for inferiority, self-hatred, or false guilt. Rather, the Presentation of Jesus reminds us that we are *wanted*. We are received and reverenced. There is no such thing as a life unworthy of life in the eyes of the One in whose image we are made. Each life is cherished by God. No one who comes to the Lord is ever rejected.

The Presentation of Jesus in the Temple is anything but a passive religious ritual. Yes, we are wanted and accepted by God. But there is more. We are also *sent*. For the gift of life carries with it expectations about how we live and the kind of people we become. The Holy Family will leave the Temple and return to Nazareth. So it is with each of us. We leave our churches and return to the everyday as "candles of the Lord." We shine as signs of contradiction. Life is a gift. We are wanted. And we are worthy of the Lord's expectations.

Spend a few moments in quiet prayer. Call to mind various ways in which you have felt the acceptance of God and the rejection of the world. Write your response to the following questions.

What are some of the major symbols of power in the modern world? How do they hinder our acknowledgment of God?

_____

_____

_____

23

In what ways have you felt accepted and totally loved by God? How have these moments of grace enriched your spiritual life?

_____

_____

_____

In what ways have you felt the rejection and hostility of the world in living the Gospel? How have you responded to such hostility?

_____

_____

_____

How do you present the Gospel to the world in your daily life? How do you try to be a "candle of the Lord"?

_____

_____

_____

They Returned

The Presentation of Jesus in the Temple reveals the power of grace to surprise and transcend the calculations of human beings — even the expectations of the Holy Family. Luke tells us that Mary and Joseph brought Jesus to the Temple in order to fulfill "what is said in the law of the Lord" (Lk 2:24). Yet they did not expect to find Simeon and Anna. Both of these deeply spiritual sages spoke about Jesus in profound ways. Mary and Joseph "marveled at what was said about Jesus" (Lk 2:33). The Presentation of Jesus turned into something more than obedience to the law of the Lord. It was a time of grace.

No doubt the natural thing for proud parents to have done would have been to linger in the Temple and bask in the glory of the moment. However, Luke tells us "when they had performed everything according to the law of the Lord, they returned to Galilee, to their own city, Nazareth" (Lk 2:39). Mary and Joseph are not swept along by the praise of the moment. They return home in order to give glory to the Lord. For it

24

is not in the Temple in Jerusalem that they are called to serve the Lord. The Word came to them in the ordinary circumstances of their lives. It is into the ordinary, everydayness of life that they must return. Mary and Joseph, along with Jesus, return to Nazareth in order to grow in holiness. The sublime wisdom we are offered is this: each of us is called to grow in holiness in the ordinary, everyday dimensions of our lives. We are to grow in holiness in time and in space; in the everyday and in our own city.

Holiness is not an abstraction or a mere external religious performance in a temple or a church. Holiness runs through the marrow of our whole existence. What we say, do, and celebrate in church must be carried back to the weekdays and everyday places in which we live. Luke concludes with these words: "And the child grew and became strong, filled with wisdom; and the favor of God was upon him" (Lk 2:40). Jesus grew in his own town and under the everyday care of Mary and Joseph.

Spend a few minutes in quiet reflection on the everyday routines of your life. Pay special attention to those aspects which move you away from God as well as closer to God. Write your responses below.

When you hear the word "holiness" what images, thoughts, and feelings come to mind?

_____

_____

How does the call to holiness fit into your everyday life?

_____

_____

What aspects of your everyday life hinder your relationship with God? What aspects aid that relationship?

_____

_____

How do you use the gift of time to grow in wisdom of the Lord? Of special concern is the gift of "ordinary" time.

_____

_____

25

The Finding of Jesus in the Temple

Luke 2:41-52

GENERATIONAL CONFLICT IS NOT quite as new as we think. There is always a tension between the elders and the new generation, parents and children. There is a conflict between what is and what is yet to be. Parents have a definite expectation of their children. Children often go off on their own in search of stability. This is not only timely but timeless in human drama.

Mary, Joseph, and Jesus make the customary visit to the Temple in Jerusalem. However, on the way home Mary notices that Jesus is not in the caravan. Mary and Joseph return, frantically looking for Jesus. After three days they find him in the Temple, engaging the best religious and legal minds of the day in discussion.

The face of Mary says so much. There is a joy and relief at finding Jesus. However this quickly becomes a righteous anger: "Son, why have you scared me and your father nearly to death?" No doubt these words came out with an edge that conveyed anger, concern, and bewilderment. Yes, Mary was glad to find Jesus. But like any mother she wanted to let him know that such behavior was unacceptable. Notice how Mary's hands come together to express her inner tension between joy and anger. Joseph continues his supportive presence. His hands serve as powerful, silent support to a mother and wife who is ready to explode.

Mary finally regains control. Yet Jesus must have his say: "Mother, I must spend time in the Temple so that I can prepare for my life's work." St. Luke captures the humanity of this episode with an elegant simplicity: Mary and Joseph didn't understand the response of Jesus. Yet he must remain obedient to them. Mary treasures all this in her heart. Jesus grows in maturity. Life goes on. Yet there is anxiety and misunderstanding. Life goes on.

Spend a few moments in quiet prayer. Carefully read the story of the finding of Jesus in the Temple. Write your responses to the following questions.

Reflect on the illustration of the finding of Jesus in the Temple. Write your reflections about each of the figures represented in the illustration.

Mary

_____

_____

_____

_____

_____

_____

Joseph

_____

_____

_____

_____

_____

_____

Jesus

_____

_____

_____

_____

_____

_____

Teachers

_____

_____

_____

_____

In what ways have you experienced the generation conflict? What are the spiritual dimensions of this tension?

_____

_____

_____

_____

What can we learn from the Holy Family in terms of coping with generational tension? What role did Joseph play in helping Jesus grow in maturity?

_____

_____

_____

_____

Why?

We humans are never quite satisfied with the "facts" of a situation; the "whatness" of an episode. We want to know *why*. There is within us the drive not only for knowledge; we desire wisdom. Even in a culture which dismisses the metaphysical and transcendent, there is an enduring fascination with the deeper dimensions of the ordinary and familiar. For example, in honor of the anniversary of Columbus' arrival in the New World, NASA launched a project known as SETI (Search for Extraterrestrial

Intelligence). Radio-telescopes are searching the heavens for intelligent life. There is a powerful belief that we are not alone in the universe. In popular culture, ET continues to fascinate and excite our imagination. We simply do not accept things as they are. We continue to ask questions. We want to know why.

Jesus gets separated from his parents. In a panic, Mary and Joseph return to Jerusalem. After three days of frantic searching they find Jesus in the Temple. Relief is mixed with astonishment and anger. There is a sense of great joy that Jesus is safe. There is a sense of amazement that Jesus is listening to and questioning the teachers of the Law. And there is anger that Jesus has caused such high anxiety for his parents. Mary says, "Son, why have you treated us so? Behold, your father and I have been looking for you anxiously" (Lk 2:48). Mary is a good Jewish mother. Mary wants to know what is the deeper meaning, the why, of Jesus' seeming indifference to his parents.

Jesus answers, "How is it that you sought me? Did you not know that I have to concern myself with my Father's affairs?" (Lk 2:49). Jesus is saying that even the deepest and most intimate of human relationships cannot claim greater importance than our relationship to the Father. Ultimately we do not belong exclusively to one another. Even less can we claim to control the lives of others. There are limits to the deepest of human loves. If true love is to yield true freedom, we must learn to surrender to God in whom love and freedom are perfected. There is a dying which comes with every separation. There is also a joyful rebirth into a deeper love and freedom with each reunion.

Luke tells us that Mary and Joseph didn't understand what Jesus meant. Faith must take over. We don't always understand completely the events of life. We must imitate the wisdom of Mary. She "kept all these things in her heart" (Lk 2:51). It is in patient hope that all the "whys" of our lives will be answered.

Spend a few moments in quiet reflection centering your thoughts on the words and feelings of Mary at the finding of Jesus. Write your responses to the questions below.

Luke's Gospel tells us of the exchange between Mary and Jesus. Joseph is silent. What do you think was his reaction?

_____

_____

_____

_____

How do you react when faced with separation and loss?

_____

_____

_____

_____

How have you grown spiritually through the losses you have suffered? What deeper truths about yourself and God have you discovered?

_____

_____

_____

_____

Wisdom, Age, Grace

Parents want so much for their children. In an affluent society we too often equate good parenting with the abundance of material things. We try to send our children to the best schools. We flood children with toys and provide countless opportunities for entertainment. We organize play time into team sports and subject children to coaching by frustrated adults. We send adolescents on summer vacations to Europe and give them cars as a rite of passage to adulthood. Too many children arrive at adulthood surrounded by the trinkets of love but lacking in the deeper dimensions of formation. The richness of a life is never measured by the abundance of possessions but by the depth of one's heart and the strength of one's character. Children need so much from their parents. And what they need most is the loving presence of their parents.

Luke's Gospel highlights the poor of Yahweh as the ones who are rich in the Lord. Mary and Joseph are among the poor of Yahweh — the *anawim*. The poor ones featured in Luke's Gospel are economically poor. They are not part of the Fortune 500, and their life styles are anything but rich and famous. The poor ones are not to be glamorized or raised to levels of heroic virtue because they are poor. It is important to remember the

31

poor ones are the *poor of Yahweh*. These poor belong to the Lord. These poor look to Yahweh to supply their daily bread.

Mary and Joseph find Jesus in the Temple and take him back to Nazareth. It is there that Jesus grows in wisdom, age, and grace. That is, Jesus develops a deeper sense of what it means to do the will of his Father. Jesus does not simply grow older but he matures as a man sent to embody the Kingdom. And there is at work in Jesus the mystery of grace.

Jesus' parents do much to aid his maturing in wisdom. However, parents — even Mary and Joseph — cannot do everything for their children. There is a grace, a power of the Spirit, which each person must be open to follow. Throughout his public ministry Jesus follows the Spirit of the Father. And this Spirit of consecrated truth will lead to Jerusalem and the Cross. Christian joy always makes room for the balancing reality of Christian sorrow.

Spend a few moments in quiet reflection centering your thoughts on your family relationships. Write your responses to the following questions.

In what ways have your family relationships helped you to grow in wisdom, age, and grace?

_____

_____

_____

_____

_____

Wisdom:

_____

_____

_____

_____

_____

Age (maturity):

_____

_____

_____

_____

Grace:

_____

_____

_____

_____

In what ways has your family grown rich in the Lord? What spiritual insights have you
learned from family struggles?

_____

_____

_____

_____

How do you balance the joys and sorrows of daily life? How does your faith help?

_____

_____

_____

_____

The Sorrowful Mysteries

I N OUR OPENING to the Joyful Mysteries the words of Nietzsche came to mind: "Why don't Christians look more redeemed?" As we turn our attention to the Sorrowful Mysteries, we might call on the legacies of two other influential molders of the modern mind — Marx and Freud. Both of these thinkers wanted to know, "Why don't Christians act more grown up?" For Marx, Christianity is an opium which numbs us to the oppression of the poor and keeps the powerful on their mighty thrones. For Freud, Christianity is an illusion which keeps us from maturing into an independent human being. Instead of using our reason and freedom, we become overly dependent on a deity we wrongly believe will solve our problems (God is simply a projection of our ideal self into the heavens according to Freud). When all is said and done, both of these intellectuals accuse Christianity of escaping the reality of suffering.

As Nietzsche overlooked the joyful dimensions of the Christian story, so too do Marx and Freud ignore the reality of suffering and death acknowledged by Christianity. And the Sorrowful Mysteries powerfully capture these troubling dimensions of our "human, all too human" condition. There is no retreat into an illusory god or a denial of suffering and death. In the person of Jesus we must confront all of the perplexity, complexity, and seeming finality of death. In Jesus we have revealed the fullness of humanity when faced with the limitations of time, strength, human relationships, justice, compassion, and the ability to save ourselves from the Crosses of life. In Jesus we have revealed to us the mystery of that alone which heals and saves — the unbounded love of the Father. But it is a saving, healing love which becomes incarnate on Golgotha. There is no cheap grace.

The Joyful Mysteries contain the hint of what is to come: Mary receives the Annunciation with anxiety; the Birth of Jesus occurs in a stable because there is no room in the inn; the Presentation of Jesus in the Temple contains a message of conflict for Jesus and sorrow for Mary; and the Finding of Jesus in the Temple is the first public display of his doing the Father's work... Such a work will be completed on the Cross.

The Joyful Mysteries are balanced by the hidden but real presence of the Sorrowful. Likewise, the Sorrowful Mysteries are not about despair and the absurdity of existence in the face of death (Camus). Rather, the Sorrowful Mysteries contain the seeds of glory and eternal life. This is clearly evident in the Fourth Gospel. For the suffering and death of Jesus ushers in the hour of glory. The glory of the Father is revealed on the Cross as Suffering Love. Such a glory comes at a dear price — the obedient death of Jesus the only Son. Jesus dies a real, human death. There is the testimony of "blood and water" (Jn 19:34). The body of Jesus is taken down from the Cross and brought to a borrowed tomb. In the words of John's Gospel, "because the tomb was near, they laid Jesus there" (Jn 19:42).

The emphasis now shifts from Joy to Sorrow; from Mary to Jesus. Through the following Five Mysteries we are drawn into the depth of God's saving love for us. There is a hesitation as we enter these Mysteries. Such a powerful love is awesome. We are afraid of being consumed in its fiery intensity. Yet God's love does not consume but transforms. The same love which proved stronger than death, lives within us through the indwelling Paraclete (Jn 17:26).

The Agony in the Garden

Luke 22:39-46

THE CLOSER WE ARE DRAWN TO GOD the deeper we are lured into the mystery of suffering. And the more we love, the more acute the suffering. God as the Suffering Lover is clearly made visible with Jesus in the Garden of Gethsemane. The mystery of God's unbounded love for us takes on a depth beyond our comprehension. The suffering in the garden will ultimately move Jesus to drink the cup that is the Cross.

The Gospel writers (excluding John) make it clear: Jesus is in agony in the garden. The deeper one loves and the more sensitive one is to God and others, the greater the joy and suffering. The agony of Jesus comes from the sin(s) of the world. It is as if the whole ugly rebellion of the world becomes visible on the face of Jesus. He opens his mouth to draw in a breath. His eyes hang heavy with a weariness that pain brings. The hands of Jesus press against his head as if to shut out the sounds of our protests against the Father's will. The humanity of Jesus clearly shines through. It is our humanity. It is the humanity which will be healed by Jesus.

The agony of Jesus is endured in solitude. The disciples are asleep. The agony is too much to bear. Sleep becomes an escape. The abandonment of Jesus by the disciples only adds to the agony. There is mention of an angel who comforts Jesus. However, the presence of human contact is missing. The hour of agony (more like an eternity) is endured by Jesus alone with himself. Yet Jesus is never really alone, "for the Father is with him always" (Jn 16:32).

Pray

There is something deeply troubling about Jesus' response to his impending doom. Judas, along with all the powerful and proper officials, is closing in on Jesus and his disciples. Certainly we would expect Jesus to call down fire from the heavens. At the very least, He could devise some brilliant plan for a rapid escape from the Mount of Olives. Okay, if Jesus won't save himself, He certainly should see to it that his followers will go free. Yet this is not the case. Jesus tells his disciples to, "Pray that you may not enter into temptation" (Lk 22:40). This is not a request but a command. There is an urgent quality about these words. However, we find ourselves wanting to say to Jesus, "But Lord, what good is prayer in such a situation? Wouldn't it be more prudent to run away?" Yet the command of Jesus remains: "Pray." And this imperative to pray is linked with the danger of temptation.

Why does Jesus link prayer with temptation; especially as he is about to be arrested? Our temptation in dealing with the world is not to pray. When faced with danger and approaching death, we instinctively turn away from prayer and try to find deliverance in the sword, thirty pieces of silver, or some extraordinary show of divine power. Jesus is saying that we must pray and trust ultimately in the God who never abandons us. Jesus not only tells us we must pray but he enters into prayer himself. The temptation throughout Jesus' ministry has been to abandon prayer and trust in his own powers and seek his own glory. Satan first tempted Jesus in the desert to abandon the Father in favor of the kingdoms of this world (Lk 4:1-13). Luke tells us that Satan "withdrew from Jesus until an opportune time" (Lk 4:13). What more opportune time than the night before Jesus is to die?

We all find ourselves in our personal Mount of Olives. We feel the impending pressure of the world closing in. We feel the absence of God. The urge is great not to pray but take up the sword or fashion some "victory" for ourselves. In such moments remember the words of Jesus: "Pray that you may not enter into temptation."

Spend a few minutes in quiet reflection. Review your prayer life; especially those times when you find it difficult to pray. Write your responses to the items below.

What forms of prayer do you find most fruitful? Which form(s) do you find fruitless?

_____

_____

_____

What are some of the major temptations you face in your everyday life? In the spiritual life?

_____

_____

_____

How does prayer provide you with the strength to overcome temptation?

_____

_____

_____

Call to mind a recent or present temptation. Write a prayer to Jesus concerning this temptation.

_____

_____

_____

This Chalice

The humanity of Jesus is present for all to see as he prays at the Mount of Olives. Few things reveal the inner person like prayer in times of maximum crisis. Our inmost thoughts and resources come to light when we are alone with ourselves and God. Deep truly speaks to deep. In times of such prayer there is no wasted energy in playing games or trying to "work a deal" with God. If ever there is a time when we are authentically ourselves before God, it is during prayer.

The prayer of Jesus is simple. There are no wasted words. There is no sheer multiplication of words in order to win a favorable response. Jesus wants this chalice to pass. Jesus does not want to face all that is to come. Who would? It is a very human thing to want the chalice of suffering to pass. We do not seek out suffering for its own sake. We do not delight in the prospect of death. In fact, we flee these evils. We do not search for the chalice which contains the frightening mixture of suffering and death; we too want it to pass.

Yet Jesus will not pass the chalice himself. All that will happen depends on the Father. This is not passivity but receptivity; not despair but trust in the One who is totally worthy of our trust. If this chalice must be drunk by Jesus so be it. However, Jesus knows that the Father will also supply the grace necessary for its completion. None of this trust in the Father implies that the anguish is suddenly removed. The anxiety does not magically disappear. Yet there is a resolution of confident hope in the One who never disappoints.

The chalice which Jesus accepts is offered to each disciple. Perhaps our encounter with the chalice is not as dramatic or intense. Yet it is no less real or demanding. In the everdayness of our Christian lives we must face the Cross. It is quite human to pray that the chalice will be removed. Jesus so prayed. However, Jesus also accepted the chalice in trusting obedience to the will of the Father. May it also be said of us. May we too have the courage to pray, "Not my will, but yours be done."

Spend a few moments in prayer. Call to mind a recent experience in which you were called to suffer for the Gospel. Write your responses.

Does it trouble you to see Jesus praying that the chalice of suffering and death might pass him by? If so why?

_____

_____

_____

_____

In what ways has the chalice of Jesus come to you? How have you responded?

_____

_____

_____

_____

How does Jesus praying at the Mount of Olives give you courage to face your trials?

_____

_____

_____

40

_____

_____

_____

Write a prayer in which you tell the Father of a chalice you face. Be sure to express you inmost feelings and the need for God's grace. Before you compose your prayer, meditate on Jesus in the Garden.

_____

_____

_____

_____

_____

_____

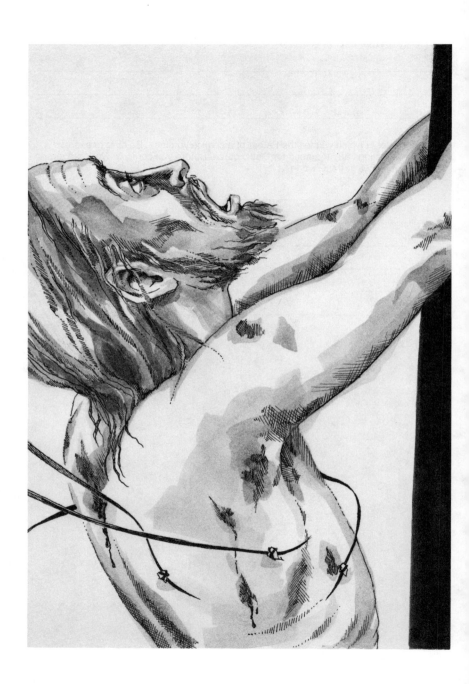

The Scourging

John 19:1

ODAY WE CELEBRATE the human body. In fact, it is not an exaggeration to say that our culture has given rise to a "cult of the body" syndrome. So much of our time is spent with dieting, exercising, and toning up in order to look firm and young. The whole cosmetic industry is built on fighting age. We crave the "body beautiful" and modern surgery hides the effects of time. Our bodies become objects of worship.

The body of Jesus now experiences the biting sting of the whip. Flesh is broken. Blood spurts out. Ugly welts become visible. The body of Jesus is now becoming disfigured. The mental anguish of the garden now passes over into the physical pain of a whip eating into human flesh. We feel the tremendous temptation to turn away. The ugliness and suffering are too much.

Yet it is at this point that faith must structure our vision and grace build upon nature. For we are invited into a great mystery, namely, that this disfigured body of Jesus is really a body transfigured into a deeper beauty seen only by faith and love. Faith invites us to see that by these stripes we are healed (Is 53:5). The ugliness of disfigurement becomes the beauty of a deeper love. Namely, the sins of the world are taken into the very body of Jesus. The Word became our poor flesh in all its weakness and pain so that it might be transformed into a living temple of the Spirit.

Pilate Took Jesus

The last resort of those intoxicated with earthly power is violence. And the violent response is prompted by fear of appearing to be weak. A prime example

43

of this all too familiar dynamic comes to us by way of Pilate's response to Jesus.

The Fourth Gospel tells us that Pilate conducted an interrogation of Jesus (Jn 18:33-38). In reality it was Pilate who found himself being questioned and put on trial by the witness of Jesus. Pilate concludes his encounter with Jesus with the cynical retort: "What is truth?" The ultimate casualty of violence is the denial of truth and the illusory belief that power can save us. Pilate believes he has no need of truth. After all, he is a representative of Rome. He has numerous soldiers at his command. In the face of such power there is no need for truth. The dictum of Pilate is simple: power *makes* truth. For the one with the power determines the truth. However, the silence of Jesus reveals the folly of such thinking. The weakness of human power is revealed in every act of violence. Once power commits itself to violence the seeds of its own destruction become clear. Why? Because the lie of violent power becomes evident, namely, that the violent use of power solves our problems and brings us into the truth.

John tells us that "Pilate took Jesus" (Jn 19:1). This is exactly what violent power does. It *takes* people and dehumanizes them by turning them into objects. Pilate takes Jesus as if he were an object or a thing to be used. The humanity and dignity of Jesus is abused by Pilate's grasping and violence. Yet what really escapes Pilate is the fact that it is his own dehumanization which he brings about. For we cannot dehumanize another person without dehumanizing ourselves.

Pilate takes Jesus, disregards truth, and reveals his weakness through the use of violent power. Jesus takes no one. He only invites us into the truth and is strong enough to respect our freedom. Pilate is a man who is in love with power. Jesus shows us the power of love. It is a power which saves.

Spend a few moments in quiet reflection. Prayerfully read the encounter between Jesus and Pilate (Jn 18:33-38). Write your responses to the following items.

What images or words come to mind when you think of power?

_____

_____

_____

Pilate ends this encounter with Jesus by saying, "What is truth?" What do you think is the meaning of truth according to Jesus?

_____

_____

_____

Why does Pilate seem to be so fearful of Jesus (read John 19:9-11)?

_____

_____

_____

What are some ways in which the violent use of power is present in our world? What can the Christian (and the Church) do in such situations?

_____

_____

_____

Scourged Him

The words stop! Pilate is a man of power and action. It is obvious that Jesus cannot be "reasoned" with. Jesus wants to play word games. But Pilate is not interested in any discourse or sublime teaching. Pilate has a problem which must be solved. Jesus is the key to the solution. However, Jesus does not want to play Pilate's game. What to do?

Pilate goes into action: Jesus must be scourged. That is, Jesus must be brutally whipped by the Roman soldiers. In Pilate's scheme of things, pain has a way of focusing the mind and getting people to follow orders. If Jesus will not be reasonable, then the reason of the whip will bring him around. However, Jesus does not respond. In fact, he remains silent in the face of abuse and the power of Pilate. This silence only makes Pilate more fearful and prone to violence.

There is a deeper dynamic at work than Pilate's resorting to power to have his way. Jesus has claimed that he came into the world to proclaim the truth about the love of the Father and his identity as the Son of God (Jn 18:37). Truth is quickly dismissed by the pragmatic Pilate. And truth is always being dismissed by those who try to deform, distort, corrupt, and make ugly that which is beautiful. Hence, Pilate must have Jesus disfigured so that he will be found unattractive and we will turn away. If Jesus can be deformed by the lash, then the truth of Jesus can be dismissed. To eliminate truth is to use violence in order to make ugly.

However, the scourging of Jesus does *not* make us turn away in disgust. Rather, the words of Isaiah are fulfilled: "With his stripes we are healed" (Is 53:5). The power of Pilate to *de*form is not as powerful as God's grace to *trans*form. Suffering and death are not eliminated, but the *meaning* of these are elevated into a higher truth. Namely, love accepts the scourging and makes it salvific: God is Suffering Love and the power of this Love shines through at the moments of greatest weakness. This is the mystery of God's love for us which can only be seen by faith. Such a love is our hope of glory.

Spend a few moments in quiet reflection. Focus on the *meaning* of pain in your life. Write your responses to the following items.

How do you respond to suffering when it comes into your life? That of your loved ones?

_____

_____

_____

_____

_____

_____

What deep spiritual truths have you learned through suffering?

_____

_____

_____

_____

_____

_____

How has God's grace helped you to accept your sufferings?

_____

_____

_____

_____

_____

_____

In what ways have you been called on to suffer for the Gospel? How have such sufferings helped you draw closer to Jesus?

_____

_____

_____

_____

_____

_____

How does God's love for you become real through the sufferings of Jesus?

_____

_____

_____

_____

_____

_____

Crowning with Thorns

John 19:25

THE WORLD LOVES TO CROWN its kings along with those who are counted among its movers and shakers. The kingly crown denotes power, acceptance, and the recognition that comes to those who get things done. The earth crowns its heroes with gold and the glittering trappings of prestige.

The world also crowns those who dare to speak a truth beyond the ideology of materialism, hedonism, and celebrity. However, the crown is not one of gold but one fashioned with thorns that dig deep into the head and heart. For those who refuse to be a worldly king, the world turns to its instruments of violence.

Into the head, and deep into the consciousness, the thorns pierce the head of Jesus. It is out of this head (and imagination) that audiences thrilled to the Kingdom proclaimed and the parables of forgiveness told. It is these eyes, now filled with pain, that looked beyond the externals into the heart of the woman caught in adultery; saw Zacchaeus as a true son of Abraham; and challenged the inner hypocrisy of those "whited tombs" filled with death. It is into these eyes and this head that thorns must be placed. For the world's only defense against those who dare to dream and see new ways (good news) is violence. No doubt the pain of this "crowned king" continues as the world still crowns its kings with gold and presses thorns ever deeper into the heads of God's prophets.

Hail King!

The irony of Jesus' being crowned with thorns and hailed as the King of the Jews is almost too much to bear. Throughout the public ministry of Jesus,

49

he was constantly being pressured to assume a political role. Jesus' miracles and discourses angered the religious leaders, concerned the political powers, and excited the crowds into trying to make him a king. Each time Jesus would withdraw. Jesus did not come to be a political leader or preach a new social ethic about economic justice. Jesus did something much more revolutionary. He proclaimed the Kingdom of God and called the people, *all* the people, to repent and joyfully accept the Good News. This is why Jesus must be discredited and disfigured. Jesus must be silenced and finally be put to death. Jesus is so dangerous because he proclaims the Kingdom of God which changes hearts and dispels the illusion of the ultimate power of earthly institutions. Jesus proclaims the Kingdom which calls all earthly values and pretensions to truth and goodness into question. Of course the response of the world is all too familiar — violence and ultimately death.

The irony goes even deeper, for the soldiers who crown Jesus the King of the Jews are speaking a truth they do not comprehend. Jesus is the King of the Jews and *all* who hear the truth which comes from his life. Yet this truth of his Kingship is not found in the love of power but the power of love. To the natural eye the crowning of Jesus with thorns evokes pity, shock, indifference, or even a sense of amusement at the plight of one who would be king. Yet to the eye of faith, the crowning of Jesus is another episode, a sign, of God's suffering love for us. The crowning of Jesus is the truth which sets us free. Namely, in the sufferings of Jesus we are healed; through his pain we are made whole; by his death we are reborn; and because of his rising we have the hope of glory.

The recognition of Jesus as King comes through the gift of faith. Such a recognition and faith does not allow us to look at Jesus from a distance. We are invited into the mystery of innocent suffering love. And when we dare allow ourselves to be one with that mystery, we see Jesus as he is. We experience that love beyond measure which makes us whole.

Spend a few moments in quiet reflection on Jesus being crowned with thorns. Write your responses to the items below.

How is Jesus the real King of the Jews and all peoples who are open to truth?

_____

_____

_____

_____

_____

What feelings are present when you meditate on the passion of Jesus?

_____

_____

_____

How does the glory and divinity of Jesus shine through his sufferings?

_____

_____

_____

What does the crown of thorns teach us about Jesus as King? Do you have difficulty experiencing the humanity of Jesus in the crowning with thorns? Explain.

_____

_____

_____

Ecce Homo

There is a strange (and very contemporary) logic at work as Pilate tries to free Jesus. Namely, Pilate believes that by brutalizing Jesus the bloodthirsty crowd will be moved to compassion and justice. Pilate seems to believe that the crowd can be turned away from killing Jesus by showing them some blood and humiliation. This seldom works. In fact, the crowd only becomes more vocal and determined to kill Jesus. The Fourth Gospel tells us that the religious leaders become enraged at the sight of Jesus and cry out, "Crucify him, crucify him!" (Jn 19:6).

Pilate is stunned and tries to pass Jesus off on the religious leaders. Pilate wants the religious folk to kill Jesus. However, they want to remain "pure" so as to celebrate the Passover! Again the Fourth Gospel tells us that Pilate only becomes "more afraid" (Jn 19:8).

Again, how strange! Pilate is growing in fear as Jesus moves closer to death. Why? Perhaps the answer lies in Pilate's invitation, "Ecce Homo!" "Behold the man!" (Jn 19:5). For Pilate is beginning to see, however imperfectly, that truth does matter, and innocent people cannot be put to death without awesome

51

consequences. On a deeper level, Pilate is beginning to see how weak human power is and how strong is the power of God's love made visible in Jesus. It is Pilate who grows more afraid. It is Jesus who is secure in doing the will of the Father.

The invitation of Pilate, "Ecce Homo," is for each Christian in every age. What do we see when we behold Jesus? The words of the prophet Isaiah come to mind: "He had no form or comeliness that we should look at him, and no beauty that we should desire him" (Is 53:2). On the natural level this is true. However, the prophet goes on to say, "I (the Lord) will divide him a portion with the great, and he shall divide the spoil with the strong... and make intercession for the transgressors" (Is 53:12). The eye of faith reveals the healing power of God's love in Jesus. The man we behold takes our sins upon himself. Do you see such a love?

Spend a few minutes in quiet reflection centering your thoughts on the image of Jesus before Pilate. Write your responses to the following items.

Why do you think Pilate becomes "more fearful" in the presence of Jesus and the religious leaders?

_____

_____

_____

_____

_____

_____

How do you see God's love and power shining through Jesus as he stands before Pilate?

_____

_____

_____

_____

_____

_____

Write a current example of violence producing more violence. What do you think is the ultimate response to violence?

_____

_____

_____

_____

_____

_____

Write a meditation on the words of Pilate, "Ecce Homo." Read Isaiah 52:13-53 and consider the relationship between the Servant of Yahweh and Jesus.

_____

_____

_____

_____

_____

_____

Carrying the Cross

Luke 23:26-31

THROUGHOUT THE PUBLIC MINISTRY of Jesus the reality of the Cross was always present. In fact, Jesus made a special point of reminding the disciples of the Cross whenever they became carried away with their own "success" or grandiose dreams of power (Mk 8:27-38). This reminder of the Cross is not an exercise in morbid religion but a call to the reality of discipleship. If one desires to accept Jesus' invitation to follow him, then he must be willing to personally carry the Cross.

Jesus carries his (our) Cross. This simple statement captures the ministry of Jesus and the cost of discipleship. When we look at Jesus carrying the Cross what do we see? A man, a fellow human being, struggling under the burden of condemnation as well as a physical burden (a wooden beam). We see a face disfigured by abuse and drawn downward with pain. Yet we also see eyes looking upward; not just toward a hill but to the Father whose will is to be done. The Crossbeam is carried with a slight upward bias. In time the beam will point toward the heavens and bear the body of the One who makes us whole.

There is no sentimental piety associated with the carrying of the Cross. There is no sign of despair or existential protest against the absurdity of human existence. Jesus carrying his Cross is an example of the power of hope and the victory of love in the face of death. With each step Jesus takes the victory of grace over sin, life over death, and hope over despair a little closer to dawning.

Weep Not For Me

At first blush the words of Jesus can strike us as harsh or just plain arrogant.

As Jesus makes his way to Golgotha, a group of women are overcome with the brutality of the moment. This display of emotion seems to be tossed aside by Jesus who tells these women, "Daughters of Jerusalem, do not weep for me, but weep for yourselves and for your children" (Lk 23:28). Again, these words of Jesus seem to be quite out of character. Maybe it is the awesome pressure of what is about to happen that prompts Jesus to say these words.

Not really. The words of an unknown religious philosopher contained in the book of Ecclesiastes offer us an insight into what Jesus is saying: "For everything there is a season, and a time for every matter under heaven: ...a time to weep, and a time to laugh; a time to mourn, and a time to dance" (Ec 3:1, 4). Jesus is not unappreciative of the women's compassion. Certainly Jesus is not belittling their show of sympathy through tears. Jesus, who cried at the death of Lazarus (Jn 11:33), is not advocating a kind of muscular Christianity which thinks that tears are a sign of weakness. Rather, Jesus is reminding the women (and us) that there is a rhythm to life and a wisdom to know this rhythm. There comes a time when tears and displays of emotion are useless. Now is such a time. Jesus is close to completing the cup given him to drink by the Father. To the eye of faith it is a time when sorrow will be turned to great joy. The tears of these women should be saved for the coming events in Jerusalem. For in the not too distant future, the Romans are going to ravage the city to the ground. That will be a time for tears, and compassion will be greatly needed.

Today we find much to weep about in our world. Jesus continues to go his way to Golgotha. Jesus continues to carry his Cross. Jesus continues to be mocked and crucified in the poor, abused, forgotten, powerless, and wretched of the earth. More than tears are required. We must have a faith which seeks justice and a compassion which moves us to action. If not, Jesus will continue to be crucified. His words will be for us: "For behold, the days are coming when they will say... to the mountains, 'Fall on us'; and to the hills, 'Cover us'" (Lk 23: 29, 31).

Spend a few moments in quiet reflection. Imagine that you are present as Jesus makes his way to Golgotha. Write your responses to the following items.

Write your responses to the following dialogue with Jesus.

Jesus: "Why are you standing here weeping for me?"

Response:

_____

_____

_____

Jesus: "Don't you see many things in your everyday world which cause you to weep? What are they?"

Response:

_____

_____

_____

Jesus: "What are you doing to help wipe away the tears of the poor and the powerless in your midst?"

Response:

_____

_____

_____

Jesus: "What are you going to do today to show compassion to another?"

Response:

_____

_____

_____

Toward Golgotha

The French existential philosopher Albert Camus presents life as essentially absurd. That is, there is no ultimate meaning to human existence. Whatever meaning there is to be found results from our own efforts. The only significant philosophical question is suicide. That is, we must decide each day whether we shall live another day or end our lives. Camus does not counsel suicide. Quite the opposite. In his masterful work, *The Myth of Sisyphus*, Camus finds his hero in Sisyphus. Why? Because in the face of absurdly pushing a rock up a hill each day, Sisyphus accepts his burden and becomes a hero.

There is no lasting meaning, only the effort of Sisyphus to face the absurdity and continue on.

What a different hero is Jesus of Nazareth. There is an ultimate meaning to life because of the One who is ultimate truth. The only absurdity and disillusionment is the persistent belief in disillusionment (T.S. Eliot). Jesus is not pushing a rock up a hill. Jesus is carrying the Cross to Golgotha in obedient love for the will of the Father. The natural eye sees a man crushed beneath the weight of his burden. The natural eye sees a journey to futility ending in death. The natural eye sees only a man abandoned by everyone he trusted and powerless in the face of forces beyond his control. Yet to the eye of faith we see the God-man who is noble in his mission and moves towards a death which will bring forth life. The eye of faith recognizes the futility of trusting in human powers and the only hope of glory coming from the Father. Jesus is the hero beyond the heroic because He loves so completely. Sisyphus moves his rock to the hill out of sheer willfulness and pride. Jesus accepts the Cross toward Golgotha out of love. And it is on the hill where Jesus dies that we are all born anew.

Each of us must decide which path to take, which burden to assume, and which figure to follow. There is something attractively romantic about Sisyphus pushing his burden with a resolute determination to conquer. However, in the end the rock returns to the bottom once more. It is only in Jesus that the burden is transformed from death to life; absurdity to truth. And this is done because only in Jesus do we find the love which saves.

Spend a few moments in quiet reflection. Imagine you are a spectator as Jesus passes carrying his Cross. Write your response to the following items.

Do you experience the absurdity of life at times? Explain. How do you overcome such feelings?

_____

_____

_____

_____

_____

_____

What do you find attractive about Camus' philosophy of life? Do you ever feel like Sisyphus? What particular burden is pressing on you at this time?

_____

_____

_____

In what ways do you minister to those who feel that life is meaningless?

_____

_____

_____

_____

_____

In what ways does the Passion of Jesus give you encouragement in carrying your own personal Cross?

_____

_____

_____

_____

_____

The Crucifixion

Luke 23:32-46;   John 19:25-30

THE APOSTLE OF THE NEW TESTAMENT mocks death by asking where is its sting and victory (1 Cor 15:55). The poet warns death not to be proud for life has triumphed. Yet these words seem quite unreal at this moment when Jesus is nailed to the Cross. The disciples have all fled. The power of the world is most evident and seems supreme. The work of the last three years would appear to be swallowed up in the defeat of the Cross. Golgotha appears to be anything but a victory. Jesus has been handed over to the righteous and powerful. He has been abandoned by friends and God. The love of power has triumphed over the One who came proclaiming the power of love.

We cannot look at Jesus directly. It is as if we must distance ourselves from the Man of Sorrows who became sin for our sake. We seem to need the distance in order to make sense of this mystery of love. For that is exactly what the crucifixion of Jesus is: the mystery of God's unbounded love for us. This love is too deep and demanding for us to engage head on. We must come at Jesus on the Cross from an angle. The full weight of this love is too much for us to bear.

Jesus dies a real human death. Life ends. Breathing stops. Blood no longer moves through the veins. The body is still. The mind ceases to function. The eyes close. The head is bowed. The spirit is given up *and handed over* (Jn 19:30). The end is here. So also is the new beginning!

61

Forgiveness

Once again we are indebted to St. Luke for the beautiful Gospel he crafted for the Church. A significant theme in Luke's Gospel is the compassion and forgiveness of God made visible in Jesus. And nowhere is this forgiving love more clearly manifest than in the story of Jesus forgiving the thief with whom He was crucified (Lk 23:39-43). Long ago in the Sermon on the Plain (Lk 6:17-49) Jesus said: "Love your enemies, do good to those who hate you, bless those who curse you, pray for those who abuse you... Be compassionate as your Father is compassionate." (Lk 6:27, 36). From the beginning of the public ministry to its completion on the Cross, Jesus is the compassion of God. He not only teaches about compassion; Jesus *shows* what it means to be compassionate. He breathes his last and hands over his spirit. There is no more fitting way to complete the work of the Father than by forgiving one of the least, lost, and last of God. Now heaven has much to celebrate: the work of Jesus is now finished and Jesus is bringing home with him a repentant sinner now born to new life.

One of the most important forms of ministry entrusted to the Church is that of reconciliation. However, we must follow the example of Jesus. We must not get caught up in questions about merit and the personal worth of those who are in need of healing. Jesus didn't quiz the criminal about his past or his sincerity. Jesus accepted the criminal and his request for forgiveness. Jesus simply tells the man that he will be with him in paradise. After all, this is why Jesus came into the world and is on the Cross — to announce the compassion of God and the forgiveness of sins. This forgiveness is not for the deserving, the well off, our friends, and those with whom we have much in common. Forgiveness in imitation of Jesus is extended to all who are in need of, and open to, healing.

Can we really practice such a forgiveness? Yes, if we are one in Spirit with the risen Jesus. In the words of the Apostle Paul: "So we are ambassadors for Christ... Christ reconciled us to himself and gave us the ministry of reconciliation... entrusting to us the message of reconciliation" (2 Cor 5:16-21). It is a message which we must share in word and deed.

Spend a few minutes in quiet reflection. Center your thoughts on Jesus as He forgives the criminal next to him on Golgotha. Write your responses to the following items.

Do you have difficulty forgiving those who have hurt you? Explain.

_____

_____

_____

_____

_____

_____

Do you have difficulty *accepting* forgiveness from others? Are you able to ask forgiveness when you hurt others? Explain.

_____

_____

_____

_____

_____

What are some of the major spiritual obstacles to following the example of Jesus in forgiving others?

_____

_____

_____

Do you avail yourself of the Sacrament of Reconciliation on a regular basis? Do you find this sacrament a blessing in your relationship with Jesus and others? How?

_____

_____

_____

How do you daily die with Christ? What do you find hardest to surrender to the Lord?

_____

_____

_____

How have you helped others to die with Christ so as to grow in confident trust of the Lord?

_____

_____

_____

In what ways have you been an ambassador of Jesus' message of reconciliation?

_____

_____

_____

It Is Consummated

The crucifixion of Jesus as presented in the Fourth Gospel tells us of the deepest of mysteries: in the death of Jesus the name of the Father is revealed as Suffering, Enduring Love. Through the free acceptance of the Cross by Jesus we see (in faith) the power of death overcome by the power of love. On the Cross the work of Jesus is consummated — finished. The Father sent Jesus to reveal his name to the world. Through word and sign Jesus did this work. The Father's name is LOVE. On the Cross the depth of the divine love is made visible. It is on the Cross that the Father gives glory to the Son for finishing his mission. In the death of Jesus there is the victory of life over death; hope over despair; love over fear; and grace over sin. The glory of the Father is shining through the death of Jesus. At the moment when sin and death seem to be at their strongest, the glory of the Father becomes visible. At the moment of Satan's power, the Son triumphs through obedience. At the moment of maximum sorrow, the joy and glory of new life burst forth.

The work of Jesus is consummated on the Cross. Yet the ministry of revealing the name of the Father as LOVE *continues* through the indwelling of the Paraclete within the community of believers. Jesus' words are profound in their majesty, for they indicate the great dignity of the Christian: "I do not pray that you should take them out of the world, but that you should keep them from the Evil One... As you sent me into the world, so I have sent them into the world... I have made known to them your name, and I will make it known, that the love with which you loved me may be in them, and I in them" (Jn 17:15, 18, 26). The Christian abides in the world and *continues* to reveal the truth about Jesus as the Son and about the Father as LOVE. How? The distinguishing mark of the Christian community is the love members have for one another (Jn 13:35).

Each day we die with Christ. This is not just a pious thought. This is a profound truth of the cost of discipleship. Each day we surrender a little more of ourselves and our securities to live in hope with the One who is our hope. We come to rely less on those powers of this age and more on the One who is Master of the age to come. Each day we die to the securities of this world so as to live insecurely with Christ. Each day we die to being in control so that we might rely completely on the One who died on the Cross and now lives!

Spend a few minutes in quiet reflection. Center your thoughts on the crucifixion of Jesus as the revelation of God's love for us. Write your responses to the items below.

In what ways do you continue to reveal God's name as LOVE in your daily life?

_____

_____

_____

_____

_____

_____

In what ways can your parish and family grow in the bonds of Christian love?

_____

_____

_____

_____

_____

_____

The Glorious Mysteries

MARY IS THE MAJOR FIGURE of the Joyful Mysteries. Yet, as we have seen throughout these Mysteries, Christian joy is always balanced by the realism of sorrow through the Cross.

Jesus is the major figure of the Sorrowful Mysteries. Yet, as we have seen throughout these Mysteries, death gives way to new life through the Cross of Christ.

We now turn our attention to the Glorious Mysteries. And in these Mysteries Mary and Jesus come together to reveal the ultimate hope of our human existence — resurrected life *now* through the Spirit and eternal life with the company of saints in heaven. The Glorious Mysteries grow out of the Joyful and Sorrowful Mysteries. The Joyful Mysteries invite us to a *living faith* in which we open ourselves to God's Word so that the Word can become flesh in our lives. The Sorrowful Mysteries invite us to a *selfless love* in which we *imitate* Jesus on the Cross. We daily pick up our Cross and follow Jesus into new life. The Glorious Mysteries invite us to a *courageous hope* in which we live now, and yet to come, that glorious life with the God of our destiny. We arrive at glory only after a pilgrimage through this world which passes away. It is not a journey of futility, but one in which we live in the Spirit. Each day we draw nearer our true home and the one source of lasting peace and happiness. We do not retreat from the demands of everyday life. Rather we engage life in the name of the Lord who renews the face of the earth and our hearts as well.

The power of the Glorious Mysteries is the power of hope. Each mystery speaks to us of hope in the midst of despair, futility, death, as well as a hope which moves us beyond all earthly achievements. The resurrection of Jesus only comes *after* the humiliation of the Cross. We must first die before we can be raised to new life. Death does not have the final word. Life is triumphant. The Ascension of Jesus is his return to the Father. There is a sense of loss which grips the disciples in the jaws of fear. Yet it is into that fear that Jesus will send the Holy Spirit to usher in the new age of grace and liberation. The sending of the Spirit at Pentecost brings to pass the words of the prophet Joel: "I will pour out my Spirit upon all flesh, and your sons and your daughters shall prophesy and your young men shall see visions, and your old men shall dream dreams" (Jl 2:28).

The Assumption of Mary challenges us to look beyond the splendor of this creation to the glory of the new creation with God in heaven. Our true home is not in this earthly city but in that City of God not made by human hands. Finally, Mary receives the crown that awaits all who fight the good fight and complete the journey given us by the Lord. There is a crown that awaits us all in heaven. Yet it is a crown made of a gold tested in the fires of a love which pierced the heart. Every great crown always comes at the cost of a great suffering love.

The Glorious Mysteries lure our vision to a larger horizon and a deeper insight into the mystery of existence. In the midst of our joys and sorrows there is the God who has experienced every one of them. In the midst of our great victories and the dark nights of the soul, we know there is a God who understands. In Jesus and Mary we celebrate the Great Mysteries of human existence from conception to death and beyond. In these Great Mysteries we are invited into the greatest of mysteries — God's unbounded love for us. It is this love which is our true hope.

The Resurrection

Matthew 28:1-20

OW LIKE JESUS TO APPEAR FIRST to those who live on the
margins of society. After all, Jesus came unto his own who
refused to receive him. Jesus is the foundation of Israel who
was rejected by the religious leaders of the day. It was Jesus who wept
over Jerusalem and longed to bring them into the new covenant of the
good news. Yet time and again Jesus was rejected or turned into some
kind of object for personal gain. Jesus continually turns to the least,
last, and lost with the good news of salvation.

On this first Easter Sunday Jesus appears to the two Marys and
replaces their fear with the words of courage and mission: "Do not be
afraid; go and tell the others to go to Galilee, and then they will see
me" (Mt 28:10). The Easter message of Resurrection is entrusted to
the women. They must go and tell the story of Jesus. They must go
and bring the eleven to the place where Jesus will appear. The new
age has dawned and the time is now for telling the story about Jesus.
Jesus is not to be found among the dead but the living. It is not a living
for this world only but a newness of life which comes from the One
who is the Lord of life.

Each of us lives at the margins of society to some extent. We are
all inadequate, by ourselves and with our own powers, to proclaim the
truth of the Risen Lord. Yet the words of Jesus to these women are
for us as well: "Do not be afraid." We are not to give in to fear which
keeps us from telling the story of Jesus. Rather, we are to be his
witnesses in all the various ways and places we find ourselves. Jesus
is with us until the end of time (Mt 28:20).

Spend a few minutes in quiet reflection. Center your thoughts on the resurrection of
Jesus. Prayerfully read Matthew 28:1-20. Write your responses to the following
questions.

69

Meditate on the Resurrection illustration. Why does Jesus first of all calm the women's fears? Why would they be afraid of Jesus? How might you have responded to Jesus at that first Easter?

_____

_____

_____

Why did Jesus first appear to these women? Why does Jesus find more acceptance among the weak and powerless than the influential?

_____

_____

_____

In what ways have you been called by Jesus to tell the story of his resurrection in your daily life? What opposition have you experienced? How has God's grace helped you to be a faithful witness to the Risen Lord?

_____

_____

_____

To See the Tomb

The subtle honesty of the Gospel writers is a thing to admire, especially in an age of cover-ups and well-crafted stories designed to enhance one's image. In Matthew's Gospel we are told that the women who came to minister to Jesus are afraid. The angel, who displays divine power and disperses the soldiers, tells the women that Jesus is not to be found in the tomb. The Crucified One is now the Risen Lord who waits for the disciples in Galilee (Mt 28:5-7). The women are sent with the first Easter message: Jesus is not to be found among the dead. The women leave the tomb with a mixture of fear and joy. Again, Matthew's Gospel maintains a realistic understanding of the human condition — the mixture of joyous fear, faith, and the nagging fear that this is just too good to be true.

The news of Jesus' resurrection must always encounter skepticism and fear. The chief priests, those responsible for Jesus' death, refuse to believe. In fact, they lie (the ultimate weapon of all who are locked in fear) and bribe the soldiers to say that the disciples stole the body. The empty tomb is not the result of God's power but of the trickery of Jesus' followers. In other words, the chief priests want the story to read: Empty Tomb Proves Nothing. Disciples Are Behind The Disappearance Of Jesus' Corpse.

Ironically, the chief priests are correct. The empty tomb *doesn't prove a thing*. But then Easter faith and hope are not the products of proof but gifts from trusting in God's word. And that word about the Risen Lord comes from the witness of others. The women needed the word of the angel. The eleven disciples needed the witness of the women. The larger community drew on the testimony of Jesus' inner circle. And so it goes down to *us*. We are the ones who inherit the legacy of the empty tomb and the need to proclaim the Lord who lives.

How do we do this? The words of Jesus before his Ascension are for us: "Go therefore and make disciples of all nations... baptizing them... teaching them to observe all that I have commanded you" (Mt 28:18). Through baptism new members become part of the Church. These new members are to live and love according to the new covenant in Jesus' death and resurrection. We need not be afraid or insecure in our calling: "And lo, I am with you always to the close of the age" (Mt 28:20).

Spend a few minutes in quiet reflection on the wonder of the Resurrection. Prayerfully read the Resurrection stories in the Gospels (Mt 28:1-10; Mk 16:1-17; Lk 24:1-12; Jn 20:1-30). Write your responses to the questions below.

After reading the Resurrection stories in the Gospels, write a brief summary highlighting the relationship between Jesus and the disciples. To be specific, what is the major obstacle to faith and how does Jesus overcome the obstacles?

Matthew:

_____

_____

Mark:

_____

_____

Luke:

_____

_____

71

John:

_____

_____

In what ways do you daily witness to the Crucified and Risen Lord?

_____

_____

He Is Risen... Go and Tell!

The message of that first Easter Sunday contains good news as well as an exciting imperative. The good news is short and to the point: "He is risen." These three little words (not the "I love you" of the romanticist) contain the news which fundamentally changed the thrust of history and the human condition. We can no longer live in the same old ways. We can *now* live in the hope of eternal life. The "He" proclaimed is Jesus of Nazareth who is now to be proclaimed as Christ, the Messiah. All along Jesus was the Son of God and the Lamb who takes away our sins. Throughout the public ministry, Jesus — through word and deed — revealed his identity as the One sent to overcome sin and death. However the human heart is fearful of good news. We resist change. We learn to love our demons. Yet Jesus announced the Kingdom and the need for conversion. The promise is worth the risk. We can let go of the past and live a new way.

The Jesus who preached and died on the Cross now lives! The focus turns to the Church in history.

The Easter message contains an imperative: "Go and tell!" The Christian community is not to remain at the empty tomb. The angel sends the women to tell the Eleven that Jesus is risen. The Gospel of John tells us that Mary recognizes the newly risen Jesus in the garden and wants to cling to him. However Jesus tells her that she must not hold on to him (Jn 20:17). The temptation to cling to Jesus is strong. We want to keep Jesus for ourselves. Yet this is contrary to the plan of salvation. The Church (the community of disciples) must go throughout the world and tell the good news. Jesus is the Resurrected Lord of *all* history and of *all* peoples. The mission is now to proclaim and evangelize to the entire world (Mt 28:19).

Both parts of the Easter message have been entrusted to the Church. We are to proclaim the good news — "He is risen!" This is the good news which offers the hope of glory and the grace of salvation to all the world. And this good news must be told, showed, and lived as a *public witness* to the Crucified and Risen Lord. The Church must step out into history and give visible witness to the Lord of all that is and will be. The Church is entrusted with the Gospel as the treasure beyond measure. It is a treasure to be shown to *all* peoples.

Spend a few minutes in quiet reflection, centering your thoughts on the Resurrection of Jesus. Write your responses to the questions below.

In what ways does the Church provide public witness to the Resurrection of Jesus?

_____

_____

_____

What special ministry does the Church have toward the poor and the powerless in society?

_____

_____

_____

What obstacles or oppression does the Church experience in proclaiming the good news of Jesus' Resurrection?

_____

_____

_____

How does the Church (and the individual Christian) face these obstacles and oppression? Reflect on the place of prayer and the sacraments.

_____

_____

_____

The Ascension

Acts 1:1-14

J ESUS NOW RETURNS TO THE FATHER and the disciples must *wait* in Jerusalem for the promise of the Father — the sending of the Holy Spirit (Acts 1:5). However, Jesus' return to the Father also means that the disciples are once again without the Lord. Their upward look and open mouths will soon give way to bowed heads and empty hearts. The disciples will return to Jerusalem and remain behind closed doors, locked in by fear.

And why shouldn't the disciples experience fear? They have left all that is familiar to follow Jesus. They remember the horror of the Crucifixion. Their hearts burned with love as they shared a meal with the Risen Lord. Jesus has been with them for the past forty days. All seemed to be well again. Now Jesus once again is gone from their sight. Jesus is on his way to the Father. But what about them?

The disciples must do what is most difficult — *wait*. Jesus' Ascension is not his abandonment of the little flock but the prelude to Pentecost and the era of the Church in history. There must be a time when the heart is made ready to receive the *Spirit*. There must be a period in which a sense of loss, with its pain and bewilderment, matures our inner being. The ascending of Jesus invites the disciples to have their hearts cleared for the coming of the Spirit. There are no quick or easy fixes. The Lord has indeed returned to the Father. There is a deep feeling of abandonment and fear. The disciples will be tested during this "time between" — between the Ascension and Pentecost.

Spend a few minutes in meditation on the illustration of the Ascension. What do you think were the main thoughts and feelings of the disciples? If *you* were present, what thoughts and feelings would you experience?

75

In what ways do you experience the absence of the Lord in your spiritual life? How do you respond to such periods of spiritual absence? Do you find it difficult to pray during such periods?

_____

_____

_____

In what ways do you see the Church struggling with the tensions of the absence *and* presence of Jesus? What changes in the Church have caused the greatest challenge to growth?

_____

_____

_____

Wait

St. Luke, in his Acts of the Apostles, recounts how the Risen Lord instructed the apostles "not to depart from Jerusalem but to wait for the promise of the Father" (Acts 1:4). And what is the promise? After Jesus returns to the Father, he will send the Holy Spirit. Naturally this fills the apostles with questions — especially about the restoration: "Lord, will you at that time restore the kingdom to Israel?" (Acts 1:6). Jesus' answer is right to the point (and one — *we* need to keep reminding ourselves — for each new generation of Christians): "It is not for you to know times or seasons which the Father has fixed by his own authority" (Acts 1:7). The mission of the apostles after the sending of the Holy Spirit is to be

witnesses to Jesus throughout the world (Acts 1:8). But for now they must wait.

It must be admitted that there seems to be very little glory in waiting. Witnessing, not waiting, seems to be the path to glory. After all, waiting seems to be so passive, timid, and fearful. Why can't we just get on with telling the story of Jesus? Isn't that what the Gospel is all about — telling the story of Jesus as crucified and risen? Such impatience is understandable but not spiritually prudent. Why? Because the Christian community is in need of the indwelling of the Holy Spirit. For it is the gift of the Spirit which gives the faith community courage, wisdom, prudence, and fidelity to the living memory of Jesus. Without the Spirit, our public witness is like the word that is received with joy but has no roots. It endures for a little while but soon falls away in the face of persecution (Mt 13:21).

To wait for the Spirit is not passive or timid. It is the prudent time of spiritual formation. Remember the disciples continue to ask irrelevant questions about the restoration. They continue to be fearful and unclear about who Jesus is and the nature of his mission. It is only *after* the coming of the Spirit that the apostles are able to go forward and tell the story of Jesus with confidence, truth, and fidelity.

Spend a few minutes in prayerful reflection on the Ascension of Jesus. Write your responses to the following questions.

In what ways do you struggle with patient, hopeful waiting in the spiritual life? Do you feel yourself wanting God to solve problems instantly? Explain.

_____

_____

_____

_____

How has waiting in and for the Spirit helped you grow in the Christian life?

_____

_____

_____

_____

Do you find yourself worrying about the end of the world or the second coming of Jesus? Why? Read Acts 1:6-8. Do these words offer you guidance or only increase your anxiety? Why?

_____

_____

_____

_____

Looking Up

Christian spirituality always runs the danger of being caught "looking up." For spirituality long has carried an unfortunate kind of abstraction which removes the believer from the daily concerns of the world and one's neighbor. Spirituality can easily slide into spiritualism — that is, an escape from history by seeking refuge in a perfect world of grace. "Looking up" is an invitation to danger *if* we also forget to "look around and within." Christian spirituality is threefold: upward (to God), outward (to the neighbor), and inward (to the proper love of oneself). The words of the angel to the apostles on that first Ascension Day should serve as a constant reminder for the Church: "Men of Galilee, why do you stand looking up into heaven? This Jesus, who was taken from you into heaven, will come in the same way as you saw him go into heaven" (Acts 1:11).

The admonition of the angel is a crucial reminder that the Church has a mission in history. That is, the community of believers must *continue* to witness to the death and resurrection of Jesus. The work of Jesus — to reveal the Father as truth and love — is passed on to the community. The world must continually confront the Gospel and the Lordship of Jesus. The world continually forgets its Lord and fashions its own "gospel" and raises up its own "Lords." Such ideology and idolatry is clearly evident in history. Wars, violence, death, indifference to the needs of others, and the quest for absolute control over life through technology clearly illustrate our maddening quest for total power and domination. History also teaches that such a quest is folly and ends in failure. The only real hope for humankind lies in the life of Jesus, the message of the Gospel, and the teaching of the Church.

The angel tells the early faith community that Jesus will come again. There will be an end to history. However, this end will not be the result of human achievement or annihilation. The end of history will come in the Second Coming of the Lord Jesus Christ. The end of history will be a new, everlasting beginning of the full Kingdom realized. For now the Church (each of us) is to witness to Jesus by the way we live, pray, worship, believe, and, above all, hope. Within each of us and the Church dwells the Paraclete to strengthen us for the journey in time toward home.

Spend a few minutes in quiet reflection. Write your responses to the following questions: What words, images, and feelings come to mind when you hear the word "spirituality"?

In what ways has the Church been guilty of "looking up" to the heavens while ignoring the needs of God's human family? How has the Church repented for such failures?

_____

_____

_____

_____

_____

_____

In what ways have you been guilty of "looking up" and ignoring the needs of your neighbor? How have you tried to put your faith into action?

_____

_____

_____

_____

_____

What do you understand the social aspect of the Gospel to be? Is this social aspect contained in the bodily works of mercy? How does the Church carry out the social dimensions of the faith?

_____

_____

_____

_____

_____

_____

Pentecost

Acts 2:1-11

THE WRITERS OF SCRIPTURE never try to hide the weakness (and attractiveness) of the human condition. After the Resurrection, and especially after the Ascension, the disciples were in a state of confusion and fear. In Acts we are told that the disciples are locked behind closed doors because they are afraid. Jesus has returned to the Father. The sheep are without their Shepherd. In spite of Jesus' words the disciples are troubled and their hearts are filled with anxiety. What is to happen next? What is to happen to *them*?

Into such hearts the Holy Spirit is sent with power and courage. At first the rush of wind and the imparting of fire only adds to the fear. What can be happening to the disciples? Are they about to be consumed? The power of the Holy Spirit is rushing into their hearts. Fear is being replaced with courage. Despair is giving way to hope. Depression passes into joy. And the timidity of being without Jesus now becomes a boldness based on the indwelling Paraclete. Yes, Jesus has returned to the Father. Yes, Jesus is no longer physically present to the disciples. Yet Jesus has returned as He promised. How? Through the indwelling Holy Spirit which now enlightens the disciples about Jesus' teachings and empowers them to proclaim the Gospel; Jesus, once dead, now lives at the right hand of the Father.

The mystery of Pentecost is the mystery of the Church born out of fear into confidence; despair into hope; timidity into the bold telling of the story of Jesus as Lord. Once again we see the Spirit at work transforming and liberating our humanity into the new creation of God's loving design. The disciples will leave the Upper Room and the locked doors. The chains of fear are broken. Hearts are set free to tell of the wonders of the Lord of wind and fire.

81

Prayerfully meditate on the feast and the mystery of Pentecost. Center your attention on the mystery of the Church. Write your responses to the following questions.

In what ways has fear kept you from witnessing to the Risen Lord? How has the Holy Spirit liberated you to overcome some of your fears?

_____

_____

_____

_____

_____

_____

Reflect upon a recent example in which you were called upon to witness to the Gospel. What fears did you have to overcome? What was the response of others to your public witness?

_____

_____

_____

_____

_____

In what ways can the Church act boldly to witness to the Resurrection of Jesus? What fears and obstacles stand in the way of such bold witnessing? Give an example of a courageous witness by the Church.

_____

_____

_____

_____

_____

_____

Humble Beginning

There is something wonderfully American about the story of Pentecost and the origins of the early Church. Namely, the Church is the story of humble beginnings sustained by great hopes in the grace of God. We Americans honor the underdog and the story of success which comes by way of overcoming great odds. Horatio Alger plays a mythically powerful part in the development of our national character. We hold dear those who are born in a log cabin and who rise to positions of prominence and achievement. We call America the "land of opportunity" because we believe there is no limit to what can be achieved by work and desire. The story of the early Church contains many of these American themes.

After the Ascension the disciples return to Jerusalem to wait for the Lord's return. On that first Pentecost the disciples are huddled together in fear. The outside world was quite unfriendly. The disciples were without Jesus and could only wonder what would happen next. Fear is a very restrictive emotion. It narrows our vision and limits our ability to hope and plan for tomorrow. Fear, above all, causes us to doubt what is true about God and what is best in ourselves. Such doubt causes us to become uncertain and to seek security in the idols of this world — material things, pleasure, ideology, religion, or power.

It is into such a situation that the Risen Lord sends the Holy Spirit. The Spirit — which hovered over the waters in Genesis; filled the hearts of the prophets; raised Jesus — is now sent into the community. The community of fear becomes alive in the Spirit. The disciples begin to speak of the wonders of God. And there is a universal effect on this first Pentecost — "every nation under heaven" comes to hear the Gospel (Acts 2:5). The division of humankind brought on by pride and insecurity (see the story of the Tower of Babel in Gn 11:1-9) gives way to unity within the one family of God. None of this is the product of human achievement, merit, or willpower (this is very much within the American story of origins and success). Rather, all is grace and the work of the God who creates, redeems, and recreates. The Church's humble beginning is really a testimony to the generosity of the Lord of unbounded love.

Spend a few minutes in quiet reflection on the origins of the Catholic Church. Write your responses to the questions asked below.

In the space provided, write a description of your images and feelings when you reflect on the Church in your life.

_____

_____

_____

_____

What are some of the earliest experiences of the Church for which you have a memory? Why has this memory remained so strong?

_____

_____

_____

_____

In what ways do you sense fear in the Church today? Why?

_____

_____

_____

In what ways do you see the Holy Spirit at work in the Church, liberating people to proclaim the Gospel?

_____

_____

_____

In what ways can the Church (and the local parish) help to bring peoples of different backgrounds (race, sex, nationality, etc.) together to advance freedom, justice, human dignity, and peace?

_____

_____

_____

Tongues of Fire

One of the most difficult and unnerving kind of individual to encounter is the *passionless* person. This is the person whose life is basically flat and who seems to be constitutionally incapable of deep feeling, commitment, or connection. This person maintains a kind of blank face and expressionless look even in the presence of the most moving news or events. Nothing seems to register with such individuals; nothing or no one is a cause for a deeply felt response. Such people even seem to lack the capacity to express an opinion. They go along with the group not because they care but rather because they *don't* care. Life is the line of least resistance and simply not making waves.

Such a life is the complete opposite of the Christian life. The Christian is on fire with the love of Jesus, the truth of the Gospel, and the splendid mission of the Church. The Christian is the person of Pentecost. He or she is the one in whom the tongues of fire rest and bring forth the fruits of the Holy Spirit: courage, faith, kindness, gentleness, and a bold commitment to proclaim the good news of Jesus as Lord. Such an "on fire" existence has no part with timidity and fear. The Christian, born in the flame of Pentecost, is about renewing the face of the earth with the truth that sets all peoples free —namely Jesus is the Christ through whom we have forgiveness of sin and the hope of eternal life. The Christian proclaims this eternal truth with zeal and an uncompromising passion for Jesus.

Unfortunately, too much of Christianity is presented with a blandness that turns the good news into dead information, Our celebration can be dry as dust. Our teachings can be mere abstractions and intellectualizing of the faith. The moral life is reduced to a series of regulations which fail to bring us close to Jesus. The trouble does not lie with Jesus or the Spirit. The trouble lies with us. We find it easier and safer to lead passionless lives — lives free from risk. We never quite leave our nets or venture into a new land which the Lord provides. However we must know this: the Spirit will never give up on us. The Spirit with those tongues of fire did not use them all up on the first Pentecost. Time and again, the Spirit comes behind the closed doors of our hearts with the flame of truth about Jesus. Wonder of wonders, we go forth in the Spirit to prophesy, see visions, and dream dreams about the great things God has done and *continues* to do for us.

Spend a few moments in quiet reflection on the work of the Holy Spirit in your life and the life of the Church. Write your responses to the questions below.

Do I find myself on fire in the love of Jesus? How does this love show itself in service to the Church and my neighbor?

_____

_____

_____

_____

_____

Do I find myself struggling with a loss (an absence) of passion in my Christian life? Why?

_____

_____

_____

_____

_____

In what ways have you been open to the fire of the Holy Spirit? Recount especially an example of when the Spirit challenged you in a very demanding way.

_____

_____

_____

_____

_____

In what way do you try to inflame others to love Jesus and serve the Church? How do you respond when your zeal is not met by acceptance?

_____

_____

_____

_____

_____

_____

_____

Write a prayer to the Holy Spirit in which you pray that "tongues of fire" may inflame
you with love for Jesus (read Acts 2:14-21).

_____

_____

_____

_____

_____

The Assumption

THE DEEPEST OF SPIRITUAL MYSTERIES are so easily misunderstood by removing all of their humanity. A good case in point is the Assumption of the Blessed Virgin Mary into Heaven. An ancient tradition speaks of Mary's being spared the pain of a physical death. Her passage from this life was referred to as a "dormition," a kind of deep sleep. Our faith teaches that Mary, after her demise, was spared the decomposition of her body. Mary was taken up into heaven when her earthly days were done. Mary's humanity is affirmed. What God did for Mary is an anticipation of what is in store for all who die in the Lord. At some point, all those who are faithful to the Gospel will be raised and joined to the Lord for all eternity. We see in Mary's Assumption our hope of new life.

What is easily lost in much of our talk about the Assumption is the fact that Mary was not so much taken up into heaven as she was *received* into heaven by Jesus. Our illustration of Mary's reception, body and soul, into heaven powerfully captures her being received by Jesus. The Assumption of Mary is her reunion with Jesus for all eternity. Mary received her Son from the Cross and took him unto herself. With her Assumption Jesus now receives his mother into the lasting home prepared for us. The Assumption of Mary is her reunion with her Son. It also serves as a powerful reminder of our ultimate hope — to be received by Jesus in heaven. We are meant for more than life on earth. Sin does not have the final word. Physical death and bodily corruption still occur. However there is more to our existence. We look to Mary and her Assumption as a hope grounded in what God has done. Mary has gone ahead of us. However, Mary is not the exception to our condition and hope; rather Mary is our encouragement as we journey toward home. Jesus receives Mary. Jesus is also waiting to receive each of us.

Spend a few minutes in quiet reflection on the Assumption of Mary into heaven. Pay special attention to the illustration of Mary's Assumption. Write your responses to the questions below.

89

Write a brief dialogue between Jesus and Mary on the occasion of her Assumption. (Draw inspiration from the illustration.)

Jesus: _____

_____

Mary: _____

_____

Jesus: _____

_____

Mary: _____

_____

What do you imagine the afterlife to be like? Do you find yourself meditating on death? How? Why?

_____

_____

In what ways does the Assumption of Mary fill you with hope? How does this hope of being received by Jesus help you with your daily Christian witness?

_____

_____

On Earth as in Heaven

The belief that earth and heaven are connected is a fundamental conviction in the Bible. God does not simply create the world and then forget the work of his hands. The Lord of creation is also the God who is active and caring in time. So great is God's concern for the happenings on earth that he selects a people to be his own. The earth and all that is in it comes from God. This is especially true of humanity. Each human being is made in the image and likeness of God. Each person is alive with the very life-breath of God. One of the terrible effects of sin is the alienation of heaven and earth; God

90

from humankind. The work of Jesus is the work of restoration and reconciliation. That is, Jesus teaches us in the Lord's Prayer that the Father's will is to be done "on earth as it is in heaven."

Mary's whole life is a living example of the union between heaven and earth, time and eternity, God and the natural order. From the first moment of her existence Mary was totally oriented towards God's will (the Immaculate Conception). With the Annunciation, Mary, in fear and trembling, opens herself to the Word of God. So complete is her acceptance that the Word becomes flesh in her. In the person of Jesus heaven and earth will be joined for the decisive victory of grace over sin.

Mary's Assumption is the culmination of heaven and earth, the divine and the human. For in Mary's whole life this meeting was a constant reality. We hail Mary because of the union of heaven and earth. In this fully human woman, in this fellow human being, we see what *our* lives are called to become — the embodiment of heaven joining with earth. For all of us in our own way and to the degree we are capable, are called to let God's will become visible through us. In the ordinary circumstances of our lives we encounter grace. In our everyday world there are countless moments when the veil of earth rises and heaven is revealed. During such moments we are reminded of our true home — heaven. Let us pray for such moments of grace when we are lifted up into the eternal love of God.

Spend a few minutes in silent prayer. Center your reflections on the life of Mary and her Assumption. Write your responses to the following questions.

What images come to mind when you reflect on the Assumption of Mary? How do such images enrich your spiritual life?

_____

_____

How does Mary's Assumption relate to her whole human life of being in the presence of God?

_____

_____

In what ways does Mary's Assumption speak to the mission of the Church in joining earth to heaven? Give some specific examples.

_____

_____

91

What recent personal experience of God's grace has helped you develop a deeper understanding of the need to connect everyday life with the will of God? Explain.

_____

_____

Hope

While love alone is the last of all the theological virtues (1 Cor 13:1-13), it is the virtue of hope which gets us to heaven's doorstep. The virtue of hope is anything but tenderhearted and escapist. Many of the modern despisers of religion (most especially Karl Marx) went to great lengths to dismiss religion as a strategy for avoiding the harsh reality of everyday life. Marx called religion an "opium" which numbed the lower classes about the injustices they suffered and the indignities they endured. Religion was about "pie in the sky when you die." However, while we live on earth, we are to be meek and long suffering. Religion became an excellent tool of the elite in society for exploiting the lower classes. Religion — really an ideology — was used to keep the mighty in their positions of power. "It is God's will that certain classes rule while others obey." Unfortunately there is much in Marx's analysis that is true. Too often religion has been (is) used to oppress the powerless and the poor. The virtue of hope has been turned into an attitude in which one suffers in silence.

The Assumption of Mary offers us a valuable insight into the nature of authentic Christian hope. To be sure, Mary is presented as one of the "poor of Yahweh." That is, Mary is the one who lacks the riches of the world. She is considered powerless and without influence in a world which moves according to money, position, popularity, and status. Mary is a woman; a young virgin, betrothed to a man with no special influence. He is a carpenter. Yet Mary and Joseph are rich in the ways of the Lord. For it is only to the Lord that they can turn for comfort and peace. It is only the Lord who is their hope.

Such a hope is anything but an escape from the demands of everyday life. Just the opposite. Hope draws one deep into life toward the One who is the deepest longing of our hearts — God Almighty! This is the power, mystery, and majesty of hope: the end or goal of Christian hope is to be with God for all eternity. All of our everyday hopes find their perfection in this one hope —God. All of our everyday disappointments find their pain in the fear that we shall be without God for all eternity. Hope hopes God. And the good news of the Bible is this: we are not disappointed. We can truly hope God and rest assured that God is ever beyond, behind, and ahead of us. Hope does not numb us to the pain of everyday life. Hope does not close our eyes to the Cross and the reality of death. Rather, hope opens us to ever deeper levels of love and commitment. Hope allows us to see the "other dimensions" of life — that is, God working through the brokenness and poverty of our existence so we can be strong in the Lord.

Mary would not be spared sorrow and the Cross. She knew the special pain that comes to all mothers — and especially to her as the mother of Jesus. Yet, through it all Mary remained faith-filled, constant, loving, and hopeful. The swords did pierce her heart. Mary did see her son rejected. She did receive him into her arms at the end. Yet Mary never gave up hope. Mary is now received into heaven as a reminder to us: heaven is our destiny, and hope is the virtue which daily moves us to that goal.

Spend a few moments in quiet reflection on the Assumption of Mary. Reflect on moments of hope and despair in your own life. Write your responses to the questions below.

Recount a recent event in which you struggled with despair. How were you able to overcome this despair? Do you find it hard to pray? Is prayer a comfort? If so, what form of prayer is fruitful for you?

_____

_____

Recount a recent experience of hope in your life. How did you experience the grace of God at work? How has this experience helped you draw closer to Jesus?

_____

_____

In what ways is Mary a woman of hope? Give two examples from Scripture. How has Mary been a source of hopeful inspiration in your life?

_____

_____

Compose a prayer drawing on the virtue of hope. In this prayer tell Jesus of your deepest longings and the ways in which grace has been present in your life.

_____

_____

Coronation

C HRISTIANS AND AMERICANS shy away from the use (and abuse) of titles. We associate pretension and elitism with the use of titles. Our very identity as a country came through the rejection of royal titles. We like to believe that "everyone is equal." From the perspective of the Gospel, we find the use of titles suspect. Jesus warns against the use of titles. Titles are for pagans and for those who seek power. The Christian must follow the example of Jesus — the example of humble service. Yet we also know that the early Church attributed many titles to Jesus (Lamb of God; Son of God; Christ; Son of David; Servant of Yahweh). These titles are ways of trying to understand who Jesus is and what he means for the community of faith.

We also attribute various titles to Mary (Mother of God; the Blessed Virgin; the Immaculate Conception; as well as various associations of Mary with her appearances such as Our Lady of Fatima, Our Lady of Guadalupe, Our Lady of Lourdes). One such title is Mary Queen of Heaven. The Fifth Glorious Mystery is the Coronation of Mary as Queen of Heaven. Initially we may be troubled by this title. It seems too royal and too much above her solidarity with the poor and lowly. Yet such is not the case. For this title is not something that is added to Mary as a crown of power. Rather, Mary is the Queen of Heaven because of her total human life lived in response to God's Word. So complete was her response to God that the Word became flesh in her.

Mary is the Queen of Heaven because she was the first and best example of Christian discipleship on earth. The title of Queen is not one of power and glory in terms of privilege. Rather, Mary is the Queen of Heaven as Jesus is the King of Kings. Both Mary and Jesus tell us that the road to lasting happiness and peace come through the power of love rather than through the love of power.

Spend a few moments in quiet reflection on the *whole* of Mary's life as a disciple of God's Word. Write your response to the following questions.

Reflect on the illustration of the Coronation of Mary. What qualities and episodes of Mary's life of discipleship come to mind?

_____

_____

_____

How does the Coronation of Mary as Queen of Heaven fit into the whole of Mary's life as a disciple of the Lord?

_____

_____

_____

What does the Coronation of Mary offer to the Church for its mission and identity in the world?

_____

_____

_____

Do you feel that the Coronation of Mary is in conflict with the Bible's presentation of Mary as the lowly servant of the Lord? Why? Why not?

_____

_____

_____

How does the Coronation of Mary offer you inspiration for your daily growth in the Christian life?

_____

_____

_____

Fully Human

In a spiritually rich little book about the Rosary entitled *The Splendor of the Rosary* by Maisie Ward we read: "Our Lady is the one complete human person in heaven. There are many human souls, the Saints — but they will only be complete as persons when at the Last Day they get their bodies again... Mary alone is a human person in heaven, body and soul: a complete human person, crowned by her Son Queen of the Angels and Saints and Queen of Men." These words are so simple and obvious. Yet the most profound of thoughts often come in the wrappings of simplicity and the taken-for-granted. Just pause to think: Mary is the "one complete human person in heaven." We must keep reminding ourselves of this reality as we celebrate the reception of Mary into heaven, for it is easy to get lost in the glory of Mary and forget her humanity. This would be tragic for us and for Mary.

Mary is a fully alive human being to the glory of God. The Scriptures go to great lengths to affirm the humanity of Mary. She is not a goddess but a flesh and blood person. Mary knows anxiety, doubt, pain, and confusion as well as joy and comfort in the Lord's will. The reception of Mary, body and soul, into heaven is *not* the negation of her humanity but its hope of glory. The reception of Mary into heaven is the culmination of a *whole* life spent being attentive to the word of God and caring for the needs of others. Mary is not excused from her humanity. Rather, she is drawn deeper into the mystery of the human person. Mary is drawn deeper into the mystery of human suffering and the love of her Son. The glorious reception of Mary into heaven is God's graceful reception of the one He chose to provide the human face for salvation. Mary's whole life of faith reaches its perfection in heaven.

Mary as the "one complete human person in heaven" points our minds and hearts to our lasting home. We are in solidarity with Mary because of our common humanity. In knowing that Mary, a human being like us, has already arrived in heaven we have cause for hope and courage. What the God of mighty graces has done for Mary, God intends to do for us. Mary's destiny is a reminder that we too are meant for heaven and life with God. We too are destined to be joined body and soul with God for all eternity. The Coronation of Mary as Queen of Heaven is a further commitment of God to the dignity of our humanity.

Spend a few moments in quiet reflection on the Coronation of Mary as Queen of Heaven. Write your response to the following questions.

What aspects of Mary's humanity are a source of courage and hope to your growth in the spiritual life? Give an example of those aspects which are a blessing to you.

_____

_____

_____

In what ways do you experience the reality of heaven within the reality of daily life on earth?

_____

_____

_____

How does Mary's reception into heaven help you live with the various crosses presented to you in your daily life?

_____

_____

_____

God's generosity to Mary is evident throughout her life and it culminates with the Coronation. How is God's generosity present in your life? How do you share this generosity with others?

_____

_____

_____

Full of Grace

Next to the Our Father, the Hail Mary is the most familiar of prayers. It has even made its way into our sports lingo: "The Hail Mary pass" denotes a desperate attempt to win a football game in the closing seconds of the contest. We often counsel the young and desperate to "say a quick Hail Mary" before the test or challenge so that things will work out. There is something within us that turns to Mary in times of trouble. Even the Beatles wrote a multi-million selling song ("Let It Be") in which they advise one to turn to "Mother Mary in times of trouble." Does all of this attention directed toward Mary take praise away from God? Do we turn to Mary just in times of trouble but pretty much forget her when things are going smoothly?

To the first question: we hail and turn to Mary because "she is full of grace" and "the Lord is with her." Mary's grace-filled life is because the Lord is with (and within) her. There is no taking praise away from God and shifting it to Mary. To honor Mary is to recall what the Lord has done for her and through her. We proclaim Mary as full of grace and we acknowledge her as Queen of Heaven because her whole life was lived for God. Each of her earthly days was spent in being open to the grace of God and service to her neighbor. Mary being "full of grace" only means that she is full of the presence of the Lord. Such a grace-filled existence turns her toward those in need. Hence it is most fitting that we turn to Mary in our need. She is our heavenly Mother before the Lord.

The second question relates to Mary and prayer. The Scriptures clearly show Mary as "the woman for others." She helps Elizabeth during her pregnancy and makes Jesus aware of the shortage of wine at the marriage feast in Cana. Mary is someone to whom we can turn for help and guidance. But Mary is so much more. Mary is a living reminder of what it means to be a disciple of Jesus; of what it means to live a grace-filled life — namely, each of us is called to be open to the Lord's word and daily be his servants. This is the greatest need we have —to be faithful disciples of the Lord's word. For, to the extent that we love and serve the Lord is the extent to which we know the peace which only Jesus can give. Even in the midst of all our trials, if we are open to the Word we are grace-filled and confident. Grace does not cancel our human nature. Grace builds on nature and elevates us to be what God wants us to be — fully alive human beings in the divine image. And isn't that just what Mary is? May it also be said of us that we daily pray to be full of grace as well.

Spend a few minutes in quiet reflection. As you reflect, pray and meditate on the Hail Mary. Write your responses to the following questions.

What thoughts and feelings come to mind when you prayerfully meditate on the following parts of the Hail Mary?

Blessed are you among women:

_____

_____

_____

Pray for us sinners:

_____

_____

_____

Now:

_____

_____

_____

The hour of our death:

_____

_____

_____

In what ways has your life been grace-filled? How have you struggled with accepting God's grace in your life? How have you responded to such struggles?

_____

_____

_____

Write your own prayer to Mary as the woman who is so fully human and full of grace.

_____

_____

_____

Epilogue

The Rosary: A School of Prayer

I T MUST BE ADMITTED THAT THE ROSARY is a problem for a number of Catholics (and non-Catholics) today. The Rosary to some seems to be a devotional leftover from a Church (immigrant) which no longer exists. Along with novenas, May crownings, and indulgences, the Rosary has served a purpose; but it is now time to move on. Some see the Rosary as a mindless devotion which brings up all that is bad about Catholic devotional piety: repetitive, non-Scriptural, individualistic, otherworldly, and sentimental. Granted, people today are spiritually hungry. However, the Rosary will not satisfy.

Yet maybe we are dismissing the Rosary too quickly. It just might be that the Rosary is a school of prayer which could meet a real spiritual need today. The Rosary is *a* school, not *the* school. No one advocates the Rosary to the exclusion of all other devotions and prayer. However, it *is* a form of devotion which can be integrated with Scripture and meditation. This is just what we have attempted to do in the Rosary Journal. The Great Mysteries of the Rosary have been integrated with art, Scripture, prayer, and faith-reflections on one's daily Christian life. The Rosary is part of an ongoing program of prayer and spiritual growth.

The Rosary is a *school*. That is, it is a form of discipline which requires an openness on the part of the student. And we are all students when it comes to prayer. There is about the Rosary a discipline which is required if the Mysteries and repetition are to bear fruit. The lessons of the Rosary, the Great Mysteries, are not understood in one hearing. The sublime wisdom of the Rosary takes a lifetime. Each time we pray the Rosary, meditate on Scripture, contemplate the Mysteries, and reflect on our lives, we grow deeper into the unbounded love of God. We must do such prayer and reflection again and again. Our whole life is bound up with the

101

mystery of God and the ways in which this mystery is revealed in the lives of Jesus and Mary. For the Joyful, Sorrowful, and Glorious Mysteries are about God's love for us revealed in the lives of the only Son and the Mother of God. This is not simple piety. It is the very center of our relationship with God and our hope of eternal life. For what God has done for and through Mary and Jesus, God wants to do for us. The Rosary is a school which can form us into the sublime truth of God.

Finally, the Rosary is a form of *prayer*. Admittedly the Rosary does not fit our current taste in prayer. We like prayers which are unstructured and flow from the occasion of the moment. We like prayers which call for us to express our inner needs and social concerns. The Rosary seems to fail on all these counts, Yet could it be that we need to make room for structured prayer? Could it be that the structure of prayer helps to focus our attention on the enduring needs of the human condition (for example "the hour of our death")? Could it be that the Rosary centers our attention on our human condition as sinners and the need we have for Mary's intercession ("pray for us sinners")? Could it be that the Great Mysteries of the Rosary return us again and again to the rhythms of human existence with God and others: joy, sorrow, and glory as well as faith, hope, and love? This is not a call to eliminate spontaneous prayer. The repetition and structure of the Rosary focus our attention on the power and wisdom of God's love for us.

To conclude, Romano Guardini wrote a wonderful little book on the Rosary many years ago (*The Rosary of Our Lady*). In this little work Guardini tells us that when we pray the Rosary "a quietly moving world comes into being, a world in which the prayer moves with a freedom that is bound only by the number of repetitions and the theme of the mystery." This true freedom comes through the practice of a loving patience. There are no easy answers or quick fixes. The truth of God, contained in the Rosary, comes to those who are open to the sublime. It cannot be forced. The "moving world" coming into being is God's Kingdom. The Rosary is a fruitful practice in the ways of that Kingdom of truth and peace and love.